Living Victoriously after Divorce

Powerful lessons to help you flourish after divorce.

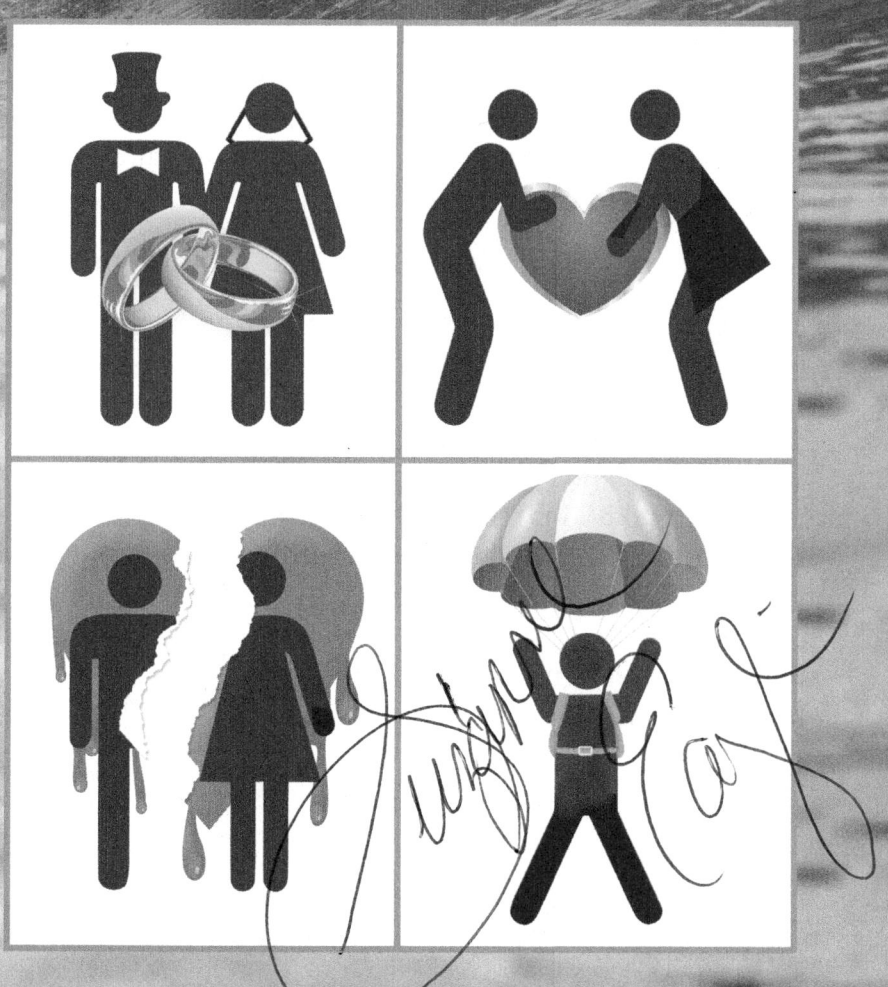

SUZÁNNE EAGLIN

Living Victoriously After Divorce

Copyright © 2019 by Suzánne R. Eaglin

IBSN: 978-0-578-48926-1

All rights reserved. This book is protected by the copyright laws of the United States of America. This book may not be copied or reprinted for commercial gain or profit.

The use of short quotations or occasional page copying for personal group study is permitted and encouraged. Permission will be granted upon request.

Unless otherwise identified, Scripture quotations are taken from the New King James Version. Copyright 1982 by Thomas Nelson, Inc. Used by permission. All rights reserved.

Scripture quotations marked AMP are taken from the Holy Bible, Amplified Translation, copyright 2015 by Zondervan. Used by permission. All rights reserved.

Book Jacket Design and Interior Layout:
Janice Gerson, DesignConceptsLA.com

Dedication

To my son Elijah, my family, and my cheer team. Thank you for supporting me during this season in my life.

Acknowledgments

I would like to acknowledge, Jerome and Tracey Carter with Inspiration 52, Morning Manna 52, Minister LaShonda Cooperwood, The Potter's House of Dallas, Bishop T.D. Jakes, Sheryl Brady, Mizpah International Ministry, Pastor Jane Wanjiku, Pastor Connie Bivens, Kathy Singleton, Phil and Brenda Martin, Lori James, Tanya James, Monica M. Henderson, Wanika Davis, True Vine of Temecula, Pastor and Mrs. Durrance and Mink Socialite Society.

Foreword

As we come to that low place in our life ... that's when we need to be reminded of the promises of God. Despite what we go through, He continues to remind us that we are victorious and more than conquerors through Him.

Every now and then we encounter a book that allows us to see ourselves from God's perspective. *Living Victoriously After Divorce* will motivate every reader. Suzánne Eaglin reassures us from cover to cover that we are winners in Christ. We are also reminded that we are not defined by our success, failures, or any other circumstance.

Thank you Suzánne for allowing yourself to be transparent as you share your life, being vulnerable enough to expose your heart and bold enough to bare your soul. This book will liberate every reader, allowing them to truly be free to live a victorious Christian life despite adverse situations and circumstances.

Once you've finished reading this powerful book, don't just sit and do nothing! It's time to start living - not just existing. Apply the biblical principles to your situation and allow God to transform your life from the inside out. There are many people who are broken-hearted and in broken relationships. This book is fresh air to a generation living like they are out of breath. Be prepared to breathe again! Suzánne has laid out the blueprint for us to live victoriously after divorce.

Pastor Jerome & Lady Tracey Carter
South Bay Abundant Life Church
Long Beach, California
www.southbayalc.com

About the Book

I wrote this book with total transparency from my own experience with divorce. I know firsthand the feelings of loneliness, isolation, and hopelessness. There were times I felt lost and endured gut-wrenching pain, with many days marred by rejection, uncertainty, and despair.

With God's strength, I was able to take back my power, make a conscious decision to be happy and live my best life. He helped me crawl out of the darkness. Now I stand in a place of purpose, power, and overflowing joy. I believe you can, too. It is for that reason I want to share my victorious testimony with you.

This book will comfort you through this most difficult season while learning how to take control of your destiny and live a victorious life. Finally, you will be inspired to reclaim your power and your crown. Each chapter offers life-giving affirmations, authentic personal anecdotes, practical, effective advice, Biblical truths rooted in scripture, a concluding prayer, and recommendations for inspirational music.

Read on, my brothers and sisters. You deserve to live an extraordinary life! Divorce is not the end of the world.

KEY SYMBOLS

  Verses taken from Holy Scripture

  Concluding chapter prayers and Declarations

  Manifestos of positive affirmations

  Inspirational song recommendations

Table of Contents

Chapter 1	My Marriage, My Divorce	7
Chapter 2	I Will Not Be Bitter	19
Chapter 3	How to Respond	33
Chapter 4	Give Me the I.V.	49
Chapter 5	Firm Grip on You	61
Chapter 6	Whose Am I?	67
Chapter 7	My Identity is in God	77
Chapter 8	Where Is My Cheer Team?	85
Chapter 9	Emergency Evacuation	99
Chapter 10	Scar Tissue	111
Chapter 11	My Weapon	119
Chapter 12	Spiritual Navigation	129
Chapter 13	Tearing Down Idols	135
Chapter 14	Temporary Season	145
Chapter 15	Living Victorious After Divorce	157

CHAPTER 1

My Marriage, My Divorce

Divorce is a difficult topic to discuss. It's even more complex when you don't have firsthand knowledge of what to expect. That's what compelled me to share the experience of my marriage that ended in divorce.

What was done in the interim before divorce was actually the conclusion. Did I pray to God for my marriage to work? Yes. I prayed every prayer I knew to pray and fasted numerous times. I wrote letters to my spouse and made poster boards writing out God's word on marriage and placed them where we could both see it. I begged for counseling and made appointments that never transpired, telling him how much I wanted our marriage to work. Did I try begging and pleading with him? Yes. I remember begging, "Please let's work it out. Please give us another chance." I even tried convincing him this was something that could be fixed. Nothing worked. There was no intimacy, even though I served myself up on a platter.

I had no pride regarding my desire to save my marriage. With desperation, I pled with family members, therapists, pastors, and other couples to help us.

We lived a short distance from a pastor we both loved and respected. I was hurt, shocked and disappointed they wouldn't counsel us. I didn't know the real circumstances as to why this pastor didn't intervene - for all I know, he could have been going through his own crisis. My disappointment only came because I cared so deeply for them. I truly loved, respected, and needed them but they did not show up.

It was painful to be in the same house in love with someone who didn't reciprocate those feelings. My husband didn't want to be bothered with me. He'd stopped supporting me and our household, leaving me to struggle with the bills while he did life on his terms. I had to borrow money to pay my cell phone bill and get gas to go to work, so I took a part-time job in addition to my full-time job to make ends meet. I don't know what he was going through because he didn't communicate with me. We were two strangers in a house, but I was still cooking and serving him meals in his bedroom. At least roommates have mutual agreements and conversations ... we didn't.

After nine months of enduring the rejection it became obvious he had chosen not to reconcile. It was hard hearing his footsteps in the house knowing I couldn't reach out to him because my love would not be returned or welcomed.

When I was a child, my dad was a provider no matter what challenges my parents had. That taught me that a man shows his love by being a provider. In contrast, my husband allowed me to stand all alone trying to figure it out. As I was fighting not to become depressed, my faith was consistently challenged, and I was lonelier than I had ever been while single.

Married but single was no way to live. I had no spiritual covering, no head of household. My husband was not my protector. I was in a house with someone who was avoiding me and not speaking to me. As hurtful as this was, I remained faithful to my marriage and our vows because God was watching me.

I would run to the window at times just to see him get in his car, as days would pass without me laying eyes on him. I had become so frustrated with the entire situation. I asked myself, "Was my marriage really over? Did my husband still love me at all? Were there outside forces that I was unaware of?"

Every day was harder than the one before. I wanted nothing more than to make up and climb into bed with my husband. Instead, I would get reports from people telling me what my spouse was doing as it was posted on social media. It was degrading, and my heart was in a chronic state of extreme suffering. I was trying to stay focused and keep a sane mind. I wondered if this was a test from God. All I could do was pray, read His word, put on some praise music, and find my escape. Every time, I felt God's love which helped me make it through another day.

When Valentine's Day came around, I bought several cards, made a poster board emblazoned with "I love you" and asked him to choose to be both my Valentine and my husband. It was on a Sunday that year. When I got home from work that morning, I put all the stuff inside his bathroom and waited. I went to my room and fell asleep, still waiting. I woke up, and he was gone. No response. No card. Our third Valentine's Day and I was alone. A friend made me aware of his social obligations. Instead of spending Valentine's Day with me, he chose to attend the party of a newly engaged couple. I was alone and he was celebrating love and marriage with other people.

More humiliation and tears fell as I skydived into misery. What type of mess was that? Who does that type of crap? How does that behavior happen and where is it okay? When do you not include your wife and pretend it is all good? I wondered how many other things existed that I was not invited to. I was on fire! He did what?! I cannot explain how much vexation I felt. This is the type of thing that could make the unregenerate me catch a few charges. I shook uncontrollably from the pain, crying all night until there were no more tears left.

On the following Monday, I completed a season of praying and fasting for a breakthrough. I remember waking up that morning with tears rolling down my face. I heard the front door close as he left. I grabbed my t-shirt at my chest into a ball, twisted it in my hand and told God I couldn't take it anymore. "Jesus," I said, "I need you to make this confusion end." I needed a breakthrough. I needed to know what to do. I needed to hear from heaven. I sent my prayer request out to prayer lines and prayer warriors everywhere. I needed a miracle. I did not see my husband the entire day.

Tuesday morning, I told my husband we needed to talk. I didn't even bring up what I knew … I was trying to move forward and not dwell in the past. Our daughter would be graduating from college soon and I wanted her day to be perfect. I wanted to make travel plans and hotel accommodations, but he told me he would be staying at his sister's house. His statement revealed that I was not included in his plans. I started talking to him about airline travel when he interrupted me, letting me know very clearly that he didn't want me to attend. It was obvious his decision was made.

I started asking questions. "Why do you not want me to come? I love her as my daughter too; I want to come." I didn't see his response coming. "I don't want to be married anymore." The pain felt like I had been shot in the heart – I just didn't see the gun he was holding.

While my heart was bleeding my mind was racing, there was yet a peace that came over me. I'm not sure he even intended to say it, but once the words came out, there was no retrieving them. I paused for a second. This is what I prayed for … an answer. An end to what we were going through. When that answer came, it was a shock to my system, forever changing my life. This was not what I wanted, so I got mad.

I started asking many questions trying to understand his reasons. When all the words had left the room, and silence returned, I felt peace again. He got dressed as quickly as he could to leave the house that day. In a short time, he was gone. I went to my room and cried, with loud sobs and lots of drooling. I was like a baby crying out for their parent to pick them up. Again, God and his peace came over me.

After nine months of physical separation, three months of separation in the same bedroom. My hemorrhaging marriage had bled out. I had done all that I was supposed to do as a woman of God. I'd heard Bishop T.D. Jakes minister one day on not staying some place where you are only tolerated. Previously, I had dealt with depression and anxiety to a degree that required me to see a therapist. God delivered me from that. Now, I was hearing God tell me, "You can return to your vomit like a dog or you can remain set free."

I chose to have a sound mind. I chose to have the peace of God that surpassed all my understanding. I didn't and still don't care what others may say or think of my decision. This is just a one-minute explanation of what it was like to be me. I fought the entire time not to give way to depression, bitterness, and anger, letting God catch and hold me in His arms on days that I wanted to just act a fool. I had to pray my way out of loneliness, rocking myself to sleep many nights in tears. I stood on the phrase, "no weapon formed against me shall prosper," praying a hedge of protection around me.

Fed up after hearing my husband's truth, I decided to pull the trigger and file for divorce. I decided it was going to be me and God. In fact, it was during the marriage when I realized I didn't see any fruit or evidence that we were equally yoked or even on common ground. Shortly after our marriage vows, my husband had stopped attending church. In premarital counseling, we had been taught practical tools to get through difficult times. But now, I could not get him to practice these strategies with me. The pursuit of keeping our marriage built on the Word of God was one-sided. It was all on me. So, when he said he didn't want to be married anymore, all those thoughts of two people rooted in the same principles came to my mind.

I refused to stay in a marriage where the roles were reversed. I know who I am, and whose I am. Therefore, I know my worth. I was not spending one more day trying to convince anyone of me being a good thing. If he would have shown effort to rebuild our marriage and keep God in it, I think our outcome would have been different.

I serve a loving God and asked for my sin to be forgiven. The sin of divorce. Some people have it much worse than

I. I know people can judge unfairly, and I know what scriptures say about divorce. I know the biblical reason for divorce, but I have grace. Staying would have been the unhealthiest decision for the both of us. Resentment, hatred, adultery – those are the things that we would have dealt with had we remained married. God promised me life, and life abundantly.

God promised me that He would complete the work He started in me. He said He would never leave me nor forsake me. I have work to do for God and being in a discontent marriage was hindering my ability to serve in ministry.

The devil had a plan for me - to stay in a marriage that would cause me to fall into a deep depression where I would cozy up to a suicidal spirit and die. You can die mentally and still be alive physically. You've seen those walking zombies. I believed God had healed and delivered me, and I was not going to let the strong man come back and bring seven more of his homies. I declined the devil's request to separate me from the love of God, and I know there is a harvest for me on the other side of divorce – a land flowing with milk and honey (Exodus 3:17).

God does not force anyone to love or accept Him. He allows us to choose salvation freely. He did not make us robots where we just do what He wants. We are not slaves. He has set us free. Why would I stay and pray that God would change the will of a man, just so I could say I have a husband? No, I would not choose to live every day in insanity. How exactly would that prayer go? "Dear God, you see, my husband said he does not want to be married. He is not loving me and protecting me. Can you make him? Oh God, go against man's will for me and force him stay. Force him to like me, love me, choose me. I know,

God, you do not make us, nor demand, nor force us to connect to you, but I am asking that you make this one man on earth love me. Thanks, in Jesus' name Amen." Uh, yeah, that is witchcraft and no thank you!

I am thankful to have loved and to have received the love that I did while married. People change their minds about commitment all the time. Why my marriage? Well, why not my marriage? God never promised that all of our days would be without afflictions. I just know that God will see us through dark days, and I am going to be remarried again one day. That is a desire of my heart. One of God's promises is that if I delight myself in Him, I can have the desires of my heart. There is plenty of loss and pain on the earth. In fact, there is enough pain that I do not choose to be one more person who is crushed by it. Being happy every day is a choice, and I refuse to allow the pain to destroy my life. There is way too much life to live. There are billions of people on this planet. If my ex-spouse and I did not make it, it is okay. I can be happy with another man on this earth.

I am happy and divorced. My ex-spouse is happy and divorced. Although my marriage ended, I do appreciate my ex-spouse for speaking his truth. I love God with all my heart and mind, and I am working in the ministry. In fact, I said yes to my purpose because of my marriage and the divorce. As a result, opportunities and the right people have come into my life for keeping my trust in God. I am reaping in places where I sowed and in areas where I hadn't. I am in the center of my Eden. What I have been created to do, I am doing and enjoy being filled with His joy and peace. Nothing can compare to that. Putting your trust and confidence in God has great rewards.

✝ *But I want you to be without [a]care. He who is unmarried cares for the things of the Lord—how he may please the Lord. But he who is married cares about the things of the world—how he may please his wife. There is a difference between a wife and a virgin. The unmarried woman cares about the things of the Lord, that she may be holy both in body and in spirit. But she who is married cares about the things of the world—how she may please her husband. And this I say for your own profit, not that I may put a leash on you, but for what is proper, and that you may serve the Lord without distraction. ³⁶ But if any man thinks he is behaving improperly toward his virgin, if she is past the flower of youth, and thus it must be, let him do what he wishes. He does not sin; let them marry. ³⁷ Nevertheless he who stands steadfast in his heart, having no necessity, but has power over his own will, and has so determined in his heart that he will keep his virgin, does well. ³⁸ So then he who gives [e] her in marriage does well, but he who does not give her in marriage does better. ³⁹ A wife is bound by law as long as her husband lives; but if her husband dies, she is at liberty to be married to whom she wishes, only in the Lord. ⁴⁰ But she is happier if she remains as she is, according to my judgment—and I think I also have the Spirit of God.*

1 Corinthians 7:32-40

Reader, let's pray together.

Lord, I thank you for being a loving Father. I thank you for being faithful to your Word. Lord, it was not your perfect will for me to be divorced. I ask for your forgiveness of my sins. Lord, I thank you for never leaving me or forsaking me. I ask that you complete the work that you started in me. Heal me, Lord, and make me whole. Let your grace abound towards me now and forever. In Jesus' name, Amen.

Declaration

I am not ashamed of my truth I use it to fuel my future.

Manifesto

Every day, I become more aware of my authentic self.

Music

Here and hereafter I offer you more songs that brought me soundness of mind. I urge you to listen to these songs too. When I felt alone and helpless, these lyrics gave me comfort and power. *To know He is with me when things feel upside down. To walk upon the stormy waters.*

Listening to and meditating on these lyrics will remind you that God carries you every day, which will keep you positive. Intentionally working music like this into your day will keep you from becoming bitter over your divorce.

>Song: "Where Would I be Without You"
>Artist: Tasha Cobbs
>Album: *Smile*, 2013
>Awards: GMA Gospel Artist of the Year, 2015
>
>Song: "Oceans (Where Feet May Fail)"
>Artist: Hillsong United
>Album: *Zion*, 2013
>Awards: Billboard Music Award for Top Christian Song 2014

A LITTLE CHAT WITH A BIG GOD

Postscript to Chapter 1

God, I have been so mad and so angry for so long. I don't want to be like this anymore. I've been mad at you, Lord. I blamed you for so many things. But I want to have peace and joy now. So, I ask that you wash me, make me new, create a new person. Forgive me for everything I've done wrong; forgive me for the blame I mistakenly placed on you. Come inside and live in my heart. Today I call you my God, my Lord, and I want to walk with you. I call you my Lord. I call you my God. I call you my Savior today. In Jesus' name, Amen.

CHAPTER 2

I Will Not Be Bitter

Your marriage is over. Life didn't go the way you planned it. Promises were made, "Until death do us part." You had dreams of raising your children in a home with the white picket fence and nice cars parked in the driveway. Now, you're hurting, lost, devastated, and completely disappointed. The depths of your soul are silently screaming, "This is not the way things were supposed to end up!" Hang in there, my brother, my sister. This is just the conclusion of one chapter. You have a lot more living to do, and God will bring you to your unexpected destination.

I too had dreams of how I thought my marriage should go. Those visions included pictures of perfect sunsets. With gray hairs salted on our heads, we'd sit in comfortable lawn chairs as our children and their children played in the backyard. Realizing that these events would never come to pass was a devastating reality for me. Thoughts of failure threatened to choke my peace. Bitterness tried to invade me, wanting me to be like Naomi who was bitter about life.

> ✝ *...Do not call me Naomi sweetness; call me Mara bitter, for the Almighty has caused me great grief and bitterness.*
>
> Ruth 1:20

I can imagine Naomi felt the way some of us feel as we're dealing with divorce. Some of you are hurting, angry and bitter. In this season, I want to challenge you to be mindful of your thoughts, words and actions. You cannot control your spouse or the circumstance. More importantly, you cannot control or manipulate God by throwing a temper tantrum trying to get your way. We also cannot hold God for ransom by withholding our affections or our service. What we can control is what we say and do. It may feel like you're alone and like no one knows what you are going through. Sweet Love, you are not alone. Unfortunately, there is a village of separated and divorced people. A village!

To remain free from bitterness, you must have a willingness to let things go and not harbor hatred in your heart. If left unchecked, a small seed of bitterness can grow. You will look up and a full one-hundred-foot oak tree of bitterness has fully bloomed in your heart. If you let this happen, you will need deliverance. Face it; the devil will take what he can get to separate you from God. If you allow a seed of bitterness in, he will gladly water that tree daily. He will watch over that seed and take expert care of it. Guard your heart!

Fictional reasons why you should harbor bitterness will cloud your mind. You will wake up to memories of things he or she said or did that will haunt your thoughts. When these memories come—and they will, put them into subjection to the Word of God. Cast them down. Force your thoughts to think in a different direction. It is natural for the broadcast of bad things to replay on the screen of our thoughts.

> ✝ *We demolish arguments and every pretension that sets itself up against the knowledge of God, and we take captive every thought to make it obedient to Christ.*
>
> 2 Corinthians 10:5

> ✝ *Finally, brethren, whatever things are true, whatever things are noble, whatever things are just, whatever things are pure, whatever things are lovely, whatever things are of good report, if there is any virtue and if there is anything praiseworthy— meditate on these things.*
>
> Philippians 4:8

The approach to the divorce process or root cause is unique to everyone. One person's divorce may have stemmed from adultery, another may have come about because someone had an addiction. Perhaps one spouse fell out of love or maybe one changed their sexual orientation. Abuse could have been the culprit. Criminal activity could have landed a spouse in jail which resulted in the split. Did love ones tell you not to marry that person? You ignored their observations because you were too deeply in love to see the truth about them. In some cases, the marriage was entered into with the wrong intentions, like personal gain or issues of control. Perhaps you may be the culprit who caused the demise of your marriage. Whatever your truth is, I'm sure it doesn't make things easier.

In some cases, we don't even understand the "why factor." Divorce can leave you scratching your head saying, "What just happened? How could I have been so blind, so stupid, so naive?" Maybe I didn't list your circumstance or cause. One thing they all have in common is, they are accompanied with some level of pain or agony.

God never intended for man or woman to live in this world alone. God's perfect plan was not for divorce. It was for us to live together until death do us part. Let's go to the Word of God and see what The Father says.

> ✝ *And Jesus answered and said to them, "Because of the hardness of your heart he wrote you this precept. But from the beginning of the creation, God 'made them male and female.' 'For this reason, a man shall leave his father and mother and be joined to his wife.*
> Mark 10:5-7

Becoming one flesh is not easy. It can also come with pain. The first few months of marriage, we're learning one another's likes, needs, and personal space, all under one roof. Allow me to share this analogy. Conjoined twins are babies born attached to one another. They share external body parts, but also share fundamental internal organs necessary for them to live. The surgery to separate them is extremely difficult. Often, one or both lives are at risk. We hear how not just conjoined twins, but other twins feel connected in other ways. They feel each other's physical and emotional pain. They can sense when one is in trouble, even if they are miles apart.

In scripture, God's intentions are evident when He uses the word "joined." Being joined to another person isn't instantaneous. By His design a couple becoming one takes place over a lifetime. That couple becomes one. When you look at one spouse, it's like you see the other. They have one sound. Husband and wife should be each other's prayer partner, best friend, covenant partner, protector, lover, and life's companion.

> ✝ *...and the two will become one flesh. So they are no longer two, but one flesh. Therefore, what God has joined together, let no one separate.*
> Mark 10:8-9

Separations and divorce are painful because you are being pulled apart from the person that you entered into a covenant with. Like conjoined twins, you're connected spiritually and physically. Let's look again to conjoined twins and the process of separation. For most procedures, it takes doctors over eleven hours, and requires a huge surgical team. The twins are put under anesthesia and the parents, even the doctors, are praying for the survival of both babies. Divorce is a similar painful separation.

Divorce is the ripping apart of two people. Often, children and families on both sides get ripped apart too. Usually, the family cannot help taking sides. The loss is real and can be hard to get over. In some cases, children live great distances from one parent, and calls and visits become less, even reaching the point where they dissipate. For all children, biological or step, divorce is an ugly monster that leaves many scars.

I still cry over the loss of my relationship with my ex-husband's family. I spent many years cultivating a relationship with my nieces. Seeing them experience life's rites of passages was priceless. I vividly remember the day we saw them off to the prom. My heart is still filled with love and joy when we just run into each other in a public place.

Then, there is the relationship with my ex-husband's daughters. Oh, how I love them! I have no biological daughters, so it was easy pouring myself into loving them. I was raised by a stepfather who loves me as his own. For me, the word "step" didn't exist. I felt the same way about my girls. I even got a tattoo that serves as a proud symbol of my love. I was not expecting to live my life without them, so nothing could prepare me for the day my telephone would stop ringing and all communication would stop. My love for them is still present and I keep them covered in my prayers.

For some, divorce is so painful that it feels like death. Your marriage died. It's worth mourning over. Do not allow anyone to make you feel or believe you should be able to get over it quickly. No one who has truly loved gets over the death of a loved one. Believers of God are commanded to love. I will never stop loving my ex-husband. However, the type of love has changed. I used to love him with "Eros love" which is a romantic love. Now I love him with "Philos love" meaning: brotherly love. It is my prayer that each of you can get to that place with your estranged spouse.

Perhaps you're hurting because the family relationship was broken due to your divorce? Do you know the name "Jehovah Rapha?" This name means, "God, who heals." Jehovah Rapha is trying to heal you from this terrible thing that has happened. Abba Father, a significant name of God meaning Daddy, is waiting for you to come out of this surgery with His peace.

During our separation, I interceded for my husband. His safety and provision were still my daily concern. Praying became a regular way of life for me. In this difficult season, I needed more of God and less of me. I could not allow self-righteous thoughts and anger to consume my life. I held fast to the scriptures, especially the ones that remind me how to love. No matter how much the relationship caused pain, no matter how much he or she may have hurt you; even if it was on purpose, God commands us to love. It's so important that He made it one of the greatest commandments. Love your neighbor. Love your friends. Love your enemies. We must love, no matter what.

God loves us no matter what dirty, sinful thing we have done or will do. He loved us and shed His blood for us. Do not let the devil make you bitter and stop loving people. If we abide in God who is Love, then we must repay all deeds, good or bad, with love. It might be challenging some days to love an estranged spouse. Do I hear a resounding "Yes, I agree"? It may take the strength of God. You will have to lean not unto your own understanding and walk in obedience and love.

Even as I write this, I hear the Holy Spirit telling me to address the sin of divorce. God said He hates divorce, not the people. He did not want us to go through the pain of divorce. Is divorce sin according to scripture? Yes, it is. Oh, but I have great news for you. Our God is a forgiving God. Ask God to forgive you for this sin. He said in His Word He would forgive our sins. He would throw them into the sea of forgetfulness. Jesus died on the cross for us to have forgiveness of sin. You are forgiven, if you have asked God. Done deal! Now we have grace. Apply God's grace to your divorce.

Here are two scriptures that address how God deals with sin and forgiveness:

> ✝ *Where is another God like you, who pardons the sins of the survivors among His people? You cannot stay angry with your people, for you love to be merciful. Once again you will have compassion on us. You will tread our sins beneath your feet; you will throw them into the depths of the ocean!*
>
> Micah 7:18-19

> ✝ *If we freely admit that we have sinned and confess our sins, He is faithful and just true to His own nature and promises, and will forgive our sins and cleanse us continually from all unrighteousness our wrongdoing, everything not in conformity with His will and purpose.*
>
> 1 John 1:9

Hatred is a demonic spirit. Hatred or not loving gives opportunity for the devil to step right on in. It will invite companion demonic spirits to enter in as well. Hatred will also cause your heart to harden. Keep the door closed and do not let this sin inside. Here are some great scriptures:

> ✝ *Love suffers long and is kind; love does not envy; love does not parade itself, is not puffed up; does not behave rudely, does not seek its own, is not provoked, thinks no evil; does not rejoice in iniquity, but rejoices in the truth; bears all things, believes all things, hopes all things, endures all things. Love never ends.*
>
> 1 Corinthians 13:3-7

> ✝ *Since you have purified your souls in obeying the truth through the Spirit in sincere love of the brethren, love one another fervently with a pure heart.*
>
> 1 Peter 1:22

> ✝ *You have heard that it was said, 'You shall love your neighbor and hate your enemy.' But I say to you, love your enemies, bless those who curse you, do good to those who hate you, and pray for those who spitefully use you and persecute you.*
>
> Matthew 5:43-44

And the second scripture, like this one, is:

> ✝ *You shall love your neighbor as yourself. There is no other commandment greater than these.*
>
> Mark 12:31

God who is omnipresent and omnipotent, sees and knows it all. He knew this day would come. He knows how sin works and how it destroys the things we love. Believe the Word of God in this moment. God is saying to you, "What the devil meant for evil, he will turn that for your good." God will use your pain, your sorrow, your shame to stable you and take you to a place of destiny that will blow your mind.

As believers, we are the light of the world, living testimonies, epistles read of men. We tell our life's story with our actions, our attitudes, and our words. Maybe someone you are dealing with has a light that has grown dim. Keep your light shining bright. Resist walking in the flesh. Be the example. Let your light shine bright, like the sun on an August day. Let it shine even at the darkest moments when you want to run, hide and bury your head in the sand.

I wanted to bury myself under the blankets and sleep until this all went away. I wanted to wake up to the thoughts of my failed marriage gone from my life. Basically, I didn't want to do any work towards my healing.

> ✝ *In You, O Lord, I put my trust; Let me never be put to shame. Deliver me in Your righteousness and cause me to escape; Incline Your ear to me and save me. Be*

my strong refuge, to which I may resort continually; You have given the commandment to save me, For You are my rock and my fortress. Deliver me, O my God, out of the hand of the wicked, Out of the hand of the unrighteous and cruel man. For You are my hope, O Lord GOD; You are my trust from my youth. By You I have been upheld from birth; You are He who took me out of my mother's womb. My praise shall be continually of You.

Psalms 71:1-6

✝ *You, who have shown me great and severe troubles, shall revive me again, and bring me up again from the depths of the earth. You shall increase my greatness, And comfort me on every side.*

Psalms 71:20-21

Do not faint. Trust in the God who has formed you from your mother's womb. Look back over your life. God has never abandoned you, and today will not be any different. He is with you amid this process. Arrest the words the devil may be speaking to your mind that are contrary to the Word of God.

Before my ex-husband moved out, we were in separate rooms. We lived in the house together separated for months. It was a daily emotional roller coaster ride for me. It is easy to catch an attitude and abide in a place of pain, but I had to make a conscious decision to not operate in the flesh.

I created exercises to help me on my journey. I took a poster board and wrote as fast as I could with a blue Sharpie, "I will not be bitter, I refuse, I am better than that." I placed it on the outside of my door. This meant I had to pass it before I stepped into my bedroom. I swear it felt like that poster was anointed by God. Looking at this sign made me treat my soon to be ex-spouse with respect.

There were times when this flesh wanted to delight in name calling and grand acts of foolishness. I will admit, my flesh got weak. Those are the moments I allowed my pain to dictate my actions and I had to repent to God. I went to my then husband and asked for forgiveness. Getting reprimanded by God was hard. I felt ashamed. Therefore, I had to make sure I didn't continuously go and ask him to God for forgiveness.

Then, there were days I wanted to recount all the broken promises of my marriage with detailed analysis. I wanted to dwell in sad emotions and allow myself to become bitter, citing, "things were never going to happen." I had to remind myself, sometimes every fifteen minutes, not to become bitter. I had to affirm, "I am better than that." Those things helped me overcome and they can help you too.

You must submit to God's will to make it out of this season of grief and pain. The devil is trying to make you play his game of tit-for-tat or getting even. Close that board game up and walk away from it, especially when acts of deliberate evil are involved.

Practical Application

- Create your own manifesto. A manifesto is your mission statement of your belief and aim.
- Surround yourself with laughter. Watch some comedy. You cannot become bitter if you keep yourself filled with laughter. Laughter is good medicine. Laugh at yourself too! Sometimes that's all we can do.

Reader, let's pray together.

Father, I thank you for your love. Teach me how to be loving even during these hard days. Lord, you see me; I am asking you to give me the strength to overcome this terrible season. Lord, I need your peace and love to wrap me up. Touch my heart, so that I am polite and kind, so you can get the glory. Help me, Father, every step of this journey. In Jesus' name, Amen.

Declaration

I am a child of the most High God, and sin will never make Him abandon me.

Manifesto

I live by God's grace.

Music

Here I offer you two songs that brought me soundness of mind. I urge you to listen to these songs too. They helped me to remember that it is not what my ex-spouse thinks or thought about me; the fact is I had to train myself to see me as God sees me. To know my worth. To be filled up.

Listening to and meditating on these lyrics will remind you of the love God has for you, which will keep you positive. Intentionally working music like this into your day will keep you from becoming bitter over your divorce.

> Song: "Worth"
> Artist: Anthony Brown & Group Therapy
> Album: *Everyday Jesus*, 2015
> Awards: Grammy Award for Best Gospel
>   Performance/Song
> Song: "Fill Me Up"
> Artist: Casey J
> Album: *The Truth*, 2015
> Awards: GMA Dove Award for Traditional Gospel
>   Recorded Song of the Year

A LITTLE CHAT WITH A BIG GOD

Postscript to Chapter 2

I feel so confused about so many things. God, I'm not sure what to do next. I have listened to my own voice. I have done what I've wanted to do and made a mess of my life. I've listened to others, but that didn't get me where I want to go either. I'm not even sure if talking to you, God, is going to work. I'm not sure if you're even listening, or real. I guess it won't hurt to try. Father God, I ask that you forgive me of my sins. Make me whole and heal the places where I am broken. Today I ask that you come into my life. I invite you to enter into my heart. Fill me up, Lord. I accept you as my Lord and Savior. I believe you are truly God, and I want to be your precious child. So, from this day forward, I submit to you. I resist the devil. Now he must flee from me. Okay, God, it is now just you and I. Amen.

CHAPTER 3

How To Respond

† *...And now this word to all of you: You should be like one big happy family, full of sympathy toward each other, loving one another with tender hearts and humble minds. Don't repay evil for evil. Don't snap back at those who say unkind things about you. Instead, pray for God's help for them, for we are to be kind to others, and God will bless us for it.*
                                                    1 Peter 3:8-9

Some of us feel like God is taking too long to move. Others feel He is running late. He should have come last week before the divorce was final. Why did God let this happen? Why am I divorced? Pastor Charles "Chuck" Swindoll says, "Life is 10% of what happens to you and 90% of how you respond."

How are you responding to this divorce? Are you using this time for discovering yourself and healing? How are you adjusting to being single? How are you conducting yourself? Do not feel inadequate - being single is not a disease. Being married, or single is honorable, and neither is better than the other. According to scripture, we are challenged to be content whatever state we're in. There are single people who live successful and fulfilled lives just as married people.

The devil loves when things happen in our lives hoping it will keep us from believing in God. Some walk away when they are hurting or grieving, citing, "I can do it without Christ." The fact that you are here right now is because He kept you. You can make it. You are surviving. You are already victorious. Do not walk away from God.

Remember, 10% of what happens and 90% percent of how you respond! In times like these, you have to just bungee jump onto the hem of Jesus' garment. In bungee jumping, the person is connected to a structure that will hold them secure while falling. You are not walking on a ledge; you are walking with God, Jehovah Jireh which means there is safety and provision all around you.

God wants us to use our faith to overcome divorce. He has given you a measure of faith according to Romans 12:3. That faith can give you the strength to move mountains. Using Swindoll's Theory, apply your faith over the 10% of what happened to you. God is able to make all grace abound toward you that you always have sufficiency in all things. Sufficiency to respond with the authority God has given you.

> ✝ *...And now this word to all of you: You should be like one big happy family, full of sympathy toward each other, loving one another with tender hearts and humble minds. Don't repay evil for evil. Don't snap back at those who say.*
>
> Luke 10:19

> ✝ *For we walk by faith, not by sight (living our lives in a manner consistent with our confident belief in God's promises).*
>
> Luke 10:19

Confusing thoughts regarding how to plan for the future after divorce can set in. These thoughts can bring on anxiety and feelings like you are about to lose your sanity. I remember being in the car driving and not realizing I was about to run a red light. How many times have you made it to work or home and thought I don't even remember driving? Then, there are those days that you parked your car at home, staying in the car because you're not ready to enter the home you once shared as husband and wife. You park, getting ready for whatever was waiting when you entered. I'm sure I'm not alone in this. I couldn't sleep at night or stay awake during the day. I know your mind and heart feels disconnected. At times, I felt like I was drowning in a sea of my disappointment, sinking deeper and deeper. I couldn't see how I was going to make it another minute. I needed God to touch and restore me. I could not live in that space.

I remember being in the bathtub just lying there feeling like my world was crushed. The warm water felt better every minute I was in it. That perfect bath that you don't want to get out of; that perfect bath you just add more hot water to. Tears began to run down my face as I just rocked myself. I felt so sad and lonely with my soon to be ex-husband only thirty feet away in another room. I began to wash my hair, and before I knew it, I was under the water. Was I trying to kill myself in that moment? No. I wanted to escape the pain. I had five surgeries in a span of four years, so I was familiar with pain. In those days, immediate physical pain felt better than how badly my heart was hurting. I opened my eyes under the water and looked up. I had a sign hanging up that said something about the salvation of the Lord. I rose out of the water saying, "Save me, Lord – if you do not get me through this, I will not make it."

✝ *Where can I go from Your Spirit? Or where can I flee from your presence? If I ascend into heaven, you are there; If I make my bed in hell, behold, you are there. If I take the wings of the morning, and dwell in the uttermost parts of the sea, even there Your hand shall lead me, And Your right hand shall hold me. If I say, "Surely the darkness shall fall on me," Even the night shall be light about me; Indeed, the darkness shall not hide from You, But the night shines as the day; The darkness and the light are both alike to You.*
Psalms 139:7-12

Being physically underwater resembled what my life felt like. In that instance, God lifted my head up and remind me that He will see me through this dark moment. I want you to be encouraged, Loved One. God will see you out of this difficult season in your life. You will recover. Stop standing in the dark looking for the light. The light is inside of you. You will overcome. Never has Psalm 139 been more encouraging to me.

I almost let go! These words were more than just words in a random gospel song. I had to make affirmations. I will keep my sanity. I will not become unstable during the separation. I will hold on with all my might to God almighty. I told my soul to be still and rest in God.

Depression is likened to a five-star hotel with many suites. The best restaurants, movie premieres running daily, great spas, and an awesome concierge service. Depression will hold you captive, and you will become so comfortable you will not want to leave, nor will you even remember making the reservation.

Once depression shows up in your life, one of its bellhops will escort you to your suite, saying, "Don't answer the phone, just let it ring. You don't feel like talking to anyone anyway. Cancel all your appointments. Quit combing your hair or shaving your beard. You need this alone time." Either you will overeat or hardly eat at all. You lose all interest, all motivation to do anything. You will find yourself questioning everything and everyone. Whom can you trust? Depression will make you replay how someone said something that one time, then take those words out of context. You will become very emotional about a miscommunication. Depression will have you make dinner reservations at the famous "Nobody Loves Me" restaurant with a table for one.

Symptoms of Depression

- Hopelessness
- Loss of interest
- Loss of pleasure/joy
- Sadness
- Anxiety
- Apathy
- Discontent
- Guilt
- Mood swings
- Insomnia
- Restlessness

✝ *For we are not fighting against flesh-and-blood enemies, but against evil rulers and authorities of the unseen world, against mighty powers in this dark world, and against evil spirits in the heavenly places.*

Ephesians 6:12

✝ *We are pressed on every side by troubles, but we are not crushed. We are perplexed, but not driven to despair.*

2 Corinthian 4:8

You may have to pray your way out of depression. If you can't find the strength, ask others to intercede for you until you can pray for yourself. Do not be ashamed to ask for someone to hold your hand. Ask for a hug or give one to a friend. Everyone needs an 'Atta boy! A dap it up! A high five moment!

We need the body of Christ to help us during the darkest moments of our life. Pray for God to send you a mentor of the same sex to help you stand. Ask God to send you a person who will be your Ruth (Found in the Bible "*The Book of Ruth*"). This person will see you through your moment. A friend who will stick closer to you than a brother. Also, I encourage you to read the Bible from cover to cover more than once for encouragement.

Now let's get more into the 90% reaction. The "what you do" part. Do not make a reservation at Depression's Loneliness Suites. Cancel your room now! It is a new day. Now, what are you doing for God? It's time to get busy working in the Kingdom! There is so much joy in serving God. Being used by God brings me a feeling in my heart that does not compare to any earthly experience. With that said, join the choir or start a Bible study in your home. Volunteer to feed the homeless. Use your talents and gifts. Use your abilities to change someone's life. Ask God to use you for something greater. Pastor Sheryl Brady taught a message that helped me so much. She said, "What you are losing with, someone else can take and win with." It made me change my perspective on life

No matter how bad you have it, or how bad you feel, there is someone in this world worse off than you. They are wishing all they were crying about was divorce, losing real estate, or having bad credit. Participate in your life. Make yourself available to be used by God. Do not let distractions keep you from being a vessel God uses for His kingdom. Allow God to get the glory out of your life.

What are you doing with what God has given you? There is always something you can do. Intercede in prayer for others while you are going through your own storm. Help a single parent. Buy someone a bag of groceries. Give someone an encouraging word. Mentor some kids. Help the elderly. Foster a child. Give aid to the widows. Doing something for others will take some of the focus off what you have going on. You cannot beat God in giving. As you give, it will be given to you—good measure, pressed down, shaken together, and running over. I am a firm believer that what you make happen for someone, God will make happen for you. In other words, while you're being a blessing to someone else, God will release a blessing to you. Your pain has purpose. Take your tears and turn them into someone's blessing. Be a blessing that is running over.

> ✝ *A generous person will prosper; whoever refreshes others will be refreshed.*
> Proverbs 11:25

Divorce will not destroy you. Never give up. Never give in to defeat. Do things on purpose that gives God glory and honors Him. You will find yourself doing activities with your 90%. This is how we should respond. Do what you have been purposed to do. Make your haters see you are more than a conqueror. The world is expecting you to fall apart. I declare by the power of God, that you will not fall apart. You will rise with Godly power and authority to be mightily used by God.

† *You shall live and declare the glorious works of the Lord.*

Psalms 118:17

† *So, whether you eat or drink or whatever you do, do it all for the glory of God.*

1 Corinthians 10:31

† *Yet in all these things we are more than conquerors and gain an overwhelming victory through Him who loved us so much that He died for us. For I am convinced and continue to be convinced—beyond any doubt that neither death, nor life, nor angels, nor principalities, nor things present and threatening, nor things to come, nor powers, nor height, nor depth, nor any other created thing, will be able to separate us from the unlimited love of God, which is in Christ Jesus our Lord.*

Romans 8:37-39

† *Therefore, see that you walk carefully living life with honor, purpose, and courage; shunning those who tolerate and enable evil, not as the unwise, but as wise sensible, intelligent, discerning people, making the very most of your time on earth, recognizing and taking advantage of each opportunity and using*

> *it with wisdom and diligence, because the days are filled with evil. Therefore, do not be foolish and thought-less, but understand and firmly grasp what the will of the Lord is.*
>
> Ephesian 5:16-17

Spread the gospel of Jesus. Go to all the earth and share how good your God is. Sing a new song. Smile and shower people with love. Acts of kindness go a long way. Count your blessings by writing a gratitude list. Let thanksgiving be rooted in your heart. Think of friends and family who have been a blessing to you. Thank them for what they did for you. Give them a telephone call or a card. Think about how something positive came out of something that was negative. Be thankful for each new day. Waking up is a real blessing. Health, physical abilities, shelter, food, and clothes are all things to have gratitude for. This will make you feel good.

> ✝ *And whatever you do, do it heartily, as to the Lord and not to men.*
>
> Colossians 3:23

I am a naturally happy person. When I walk into my job, I am smiling and flying like a butterfly. I have people around who are not morning people and are not ready for my level of excitement for the day. Listen friend, my mind set is that this is the day that the Lord has made, and I will rejoice and be glad in it. I am just glad to be alive. Furthermore, I am confident that my life ends with both victory and Godly abundance. I will not let the 10% cause me to forget the goodness of God.

> ✝ *Let your light so shine before men, that they may see your good works and glorify your Father in heaven.*
> Matthew 5:16

God is too good to us for us to act like this one chapter of life is worth more than salvation. It is by grace we are saved. God loves us so much. He has been so faithful to us. Do not let all the beautiful things in your life be discarded because of divorce.

I pray you realize that God's grace and mercy are new every morning. God's favor surrounds you. He has made a deposit inside of you with a measure of His faith. Take your faith and move some mountains. Take your faith and pray for someone. Pray for someone else to buy a house or for their kids to go to college. Do something to help others. Stay focused even during divorce. You are a member of the body of Christ. Get on your post and get active.

> ✝ *Through the Lord's mercies we are not consumed, Because His compassions fail not. They are new every morning; Great is Your faithfulness. "The Lord is my portion," says my soul, "Therefore I hope in Him.*
> Lamentations 3:22-24

> ✝ *For You, O Lord, will bless the righteous; With favor You will surround him as with a shield.*
> Psalms 5:12

Divorce is a small part of what is going on in the world. Put God on the throne and serve the King of Kings. Put a smile on your face, for God is with you. Spend time in God's Word. Put on the whole armor of God. Pray the

Word over your life daily. Live like you've been redeemed by the blood of the Lamb. Wake up! The hope of glory lives inside of you. Plead the blood of Jesus over your day. Speak to your day and tell your day it is going to be great. This day I win. This day I have the peace of God. This day the joy of the Lord is my strength. This day I will run and not grow weary. This day I will defeat the enemy. Declare that every day will be greater and sweeter than the one before. I encourage you to take the time to read the Bible story of David and Goliath.

Go find a mirror and make your confessions of God's Word over your life. You have the mind of Christ Jesus. You awoke as joint heir with Jesus. So, go do big things. Pick up your head and look to the hills from where your help comes. God is always helping, and His outstretched hand surrounds you. Stand knowing, He knows your end from your beginning; He has been counting the cost and has made a way out of no way for you. Feel the salvation of the Lord.

> ✝ *For who has known the mind of the Lord that he may instruct Him? But we have the mind of Christ.*
> 1 Corinthians 2:16

There are people out there in worse conditions than you, and they need your prayers. They need you to take your rightful place and fulfill the call of God on your life. Someone needs to see your transparency, so they can get strength from your testimony. You may be going through divorce, but the anointing is still on your life. There are numerous people in dreadful situations who need your prayers. Someone's life could be influenced if you work the plan God has called you to. It could be as simple as buying someone lunch or even a good book. Respond with acts of service. Respond with establishing the Kingdom of God on the earth. Your life is bigger than divorce.

Trust in God has to be a part of your 90% response. He is your Deliverer, grab hold with two hands of faith. When you do not see how the outcome will be, you must believe that God is working it out for your good. God works behind the scenes. He is at work on your behalf when you are asleep in your bed. He's making moves that are setting you up for your next win. If God created the earth, imagine what He can do for you.

Get physically active. Make a list of things you have been putting off. Do things you have saved for later because this is later. What are some things you want to do for you? Create a "Things to Accomplish" list. Did you want to further your education? Learn a new language, go on vacation, get fit and healthy? What are your gifts and talents? Are you using them? Maybe you have a song in your heart that others need to hear. Perhaps there is a book you need to write? Have you been wanting to start your own business.

> ✝ *A soft answer turns away wrath, But a harsh word stirs up anger. The tongue of the wise uses knowledge rightly, But the mouth of fools pours forth foolishness.*
> Proverbs 15:1-2

> ✝ *Take care, brothers and sisters, that there not be in any one of you a wicked, unbelieving heart which refuses to trust and rely on the Lord, a heart that turns away from the living God.*
> Hebrews 3:12

> ✝ *The Lord will fight for you while you only need to keep silent and remain calm.*
>
> Exodus 14:14

How are you responding to going from being a two-income household to a one income, or in some situations, a no income household? Beautiful One, you are God's child. I understand how uncomfortable it is and how you do not deserve to be in this situation. You may have to start over. Do it with strength and help from God.

You may have been the person who paid your bills on time. Money may not have been something you struggled with before. Now you look down at your caller I.D. and see collectors calling you. Do not bite their heads off. They are just doing their jobs. Be polite and respectful. You still have to represent God. You might have to get a job, or a second job, work overtime, or apply for aid. It is not the end of the world. Yes, I know how unfair it is. Take your life and respond with the declaration, "I will not lay down and die. I will trust in God. I will walk by faith. I will rebuild." This scripture reminds us to trust God:

> ✝ *Cast your burden on the Lord, And He shall sustain you; He shall never permit the righteous to be moved.*
>
> Psalms 55:22

Respond with respect and kind words. Respond by walking away from conversations that will provoke you to talk with malice on your tongue. In other words, you do not have permission to demolish someone with your quick tongue. Don't be a smarty pants! That will only feel good for a few minutes.

Recommended Activities

1. Trust in God.
2. Work in service to God.
3. Be polite and respectful.
4. Do not bite anyone's head off.
5. Do things for you.
6. Stay active.

Readers, let's again pray together.

Heavenly Father, I thank you for keeping me in all ways daily. Father, help me to use my mouth to speak blessings instead of curses. Help me to make good decisions. Teach me how to see goodness in every person every day. Help me to take charge of my destiny. In Jesus' precious name, Amen.

✝ Declaration

I speak life and blessings.

🎤 Manifesto

My mouth opens, and the ears hear love and kindness.

🎵 Music

Song: "Fill Me"
Artist: Martha Munizzi
Album: *Make it Loud*, 2011
Awards: Dove Award Nomination

Song: "I'll be the One"
Artist: Briana Babineaux
Album: *I'll be the One*, 2015
Awards: Gospel Music Awards Nominations

A LITTLE CHAT WITH A BIG GOD

Postscript to Chapter 3

I am overwhelmed. I have many complaints, and all I do is complain. I keep hearing that you can help me. I do want a better life. I deserve happiness and joy, so I surrender. I need your help. I need you to forgive my wrongdoings. Come and live inside my heart and mind. Give me your joy; give me strength; give me peace. I confess today that you are Lord. You are my God. Fix me. I don't want to continue in agony like this anymore. Take away my affliction. Lead me and guide me in your truth. I need you. In Jesus' name, Amen.

CHAPTER 4

Give Me The I.V.

With worship music blaring in my car, I was on my way to mid-day church service. The window was down, and my hair was blowing in the wind. I was having a great moment, singing my heart out. In the midst of me worshiping God, I heard a voice inside say, "Buckle up and brace for impact." I believed God was giving me a caution for what was about to come. I had a peace from God that I would be just fine. When I hear "buckle up" I think "crash." I thought about the movie, "Flight." There is a line in the movie when the plane is headed toward the crash. The pilot gives the warning to brace for safety. Only this was real life, and God was with me. This happened right before the start of my nine-month separation.

The distance in my marriage was so pronounced and I felt so desperate. I will be honest with you - as I said before, I'm a very transparent person. I don't mind asking for help or seeking counsel from someone who made it through to the other side. I knew my marriage was in serious trouble, and we needed wise counsel. That would be the only way we could make it.

Mentors are an excellent resource to help you in being successful during this season. I had a female mentor who had overcome marital problems. She was truly heaven sent.

I know her to be a virtuous woman of God, and she had a sistah's back. She only gave me Godly council, holding me accountable to God's Word, especially in terms of how I conducted myself. She would ask me questions like, "What do you want?" and "What are you confessing?"

Before marriage, you could see all the evidence of him being in love with me. I loved him with my everything. He was an enigma. At some point I stopped feeling love in my marriage. The attributes of a healthy marriage became void. Love presents seasons of hot and cold. Therefore, I did not measure the strength of marriage based on emotions. I knew emotions could change tomorrow. The common interests that we shared before marriage seemed to go away once we said "I do." When he and I were dating, we went to church together every Sunday. After a few months of marriage, that ended. He had many excuses for why he didn't want to go. My mentor helped me take the focus off him and made me look deeper at myself. While looking deeper, I realized I didn't know enough about who I was marrying or what values we shared.

I wanted to get to know my husband more intimately. At the beginning, he and I were friends. We would hang out and have no issues. However, there were times that I did not recognize the man I was married to. In group settings during casual conversation, I learned things about my husband I didn't know. I do not believe his previous lack of disclosure was intentional or malicious. On the other hand, I do believe I was being introduced to the man I was really married to.

We were a progressive couple. His ex-wife, her husband and I were friends. One night on our way home from another couples' night, I told him, "You cannot let me be the only one in the room who knows less about you than everyone else." These people had endless stories. However, they were describing him in a way I did not know him to be. He had told me only what he wanted me to hear. His version was very different and way more loving. He left out a few things that I thought were important. Being caught unaware of chunks of his life made me feel like I was on an episode of "Who the (bleep) did I Marry?" Not good. As a wife I wanted to defend my husband, but how could I when I didn't know his truths?

School was in session. I had a lot to learn about my spouse. There were three versions that I had heard, seen, or learned for myself. The way his ex-wife described how their marriage ended had more than a dozen similarities to what he and I went through.

His sister's version of the man I was married to painted a picture of a loving, almost savior-type man who was a rescuer and a giver. He had been like a father to her.

One of the best orientations I received about my soon to be husband was from my son's mentor. He told me that we would make a good couple. He gave him high accolades, validated his character and his nature. He gave him the old two thumbs up. His recommendation caused me to feel safe. Consequently, I did not launch a full investigation into my ex-spouse's background. These were credible people who sung his praises. Then there were my preconceived ideas about him being a great father. I take responsibility for thinking I knew enough. I fell in love without collecting all the data.

All I can say is my marriage had lots of surprises. I would not describe it as terrible, just absent and incomplete. At times, I felt weak, defeated and depleted. I had to figure out a way to hope again. How was I going to make it another minute? There were too many thoughts and way too many distractions. This pain required divine intervention. The different ways I had tried to soothe myself was not working. I needed God to inject me with His strength— His touch to restore me.

Seek the face of God during this painful storm. Seeking Him will cause your faith to get stronger. Perhaps you're trying to figure out what the Lord God is doing with you in this season. You may have these questions, and the perfect God who created you has the answers.

This pain you may be experiencing in this season can make you a giant in the spirit. Allow God to take your burdens. I can recall days that I felt like crying. The next day I felt like fighting. I was blindsided at times. I was uncertain what I should have been praying for or believing in.

> ✝ *If any of you lacks wisdom, let him ask of God, who gives to all liberally and without reproach, and it will be given to him. But let him ask in faith, with no doubting, for he who doubts is like a wave of the sea driven and tossed by the wind. For let not that man suppose that he will receive anything from the Lord; he is a double-minded man, unstable in all his ways.*
>
> James 1:7-8

> ✝ *So, I say to you, ask, and it will be given to you; seek, and you will find; knock, and it will be opened to you. For everyone who asks receives, and he who seeks finds, and to him who knocks it will be opened. If a son asks for bread from any father among you, will he give him a stone? Or if he asks for a fish,*

> *will he give him a serpent instead of a fish? Or if he asks for an egg, will he offer him a scorpion? If you then, being evil, know how to give good gifts to your children, how much more will your heavenly Father give the Holy Spirit to those who ask Him.*
>
> Luke 11:9-13

Heartbreak was making me both physically and mentally sick. I was like a walking zombie who needed to be hospitalized to get relief from the pain. My soul was crying out, "help me" at times. Most days I was screaming, "I am in pain!" Do you remember that scene in the 80s movie, "Terms of Endearment"? Shirley Maclaine yells, "Give my daughter her shot!" It's powerful. Go to YouTube and watch it. That scene describes perfectly how I was feeling. In the movie, Shirley's daughter was in great pain. So was I, and I needed intravenous therapy. I needed an I.V. that connected from heaven down to my spirit. At the well, Jesus spoke about this type of I.V. that I needed. Everyone who does not drink spiritual water that He gives will become thirsty again. His water would not only cause me to not thirst again, but a well of water would spring up eternal life within me. [See John 4:14-13]

Fifty to sixty-five percent of our adult bodies are made up of water. If you are in a hot climate indulging in extreme physical exercise with no water, you can quickly become sick. The sickness can even be life-threatening. Water is vital to our survival. The body will start having major medical issues, not excluding death. I am not a medical professional, so my studies may not be accurate. My point, of course, is that this is true about needing God. Extreme heat makes you dehydrated and I was in a desert. I needed to drink from the well that doesn't run dry. [See Isaiah 44:3].

Signs of Physical Dehydration

- Dryness of mouth
- Extremely thirst
- Fatigue
- Dizziness
- Confusion
- Less urination and with dark color

Signs of Spiritual Dehydration

- You are not speaking God's Word over your life out loud
- No passion, no desire for God's Word
- You do not feel the presence of the Almighty God
- Doubtful, hopeless
- God's Word seems incomprehensible
- No time with God, no reading His Word, no praying, no praising and worshiping

✝ *But whoever drinks of the water that I shall give him will never thirst. But the water that I shall give him will become in him a fountain of water springing up into everlasting life.*
John 4:14

✝ *On the last and most important day of the festival, Jesus stood up and cried out, "If anyone is thirsty, let him come to me and drink. The one who believes in me, as the Scripture has said, will have streams of living water flow from deep within him.*
John 7:37-38

If you have been walking with God and hearing the Holy Spirit, the worst feeling in the world is not hearing or feeling the presence of God near you. Our spirit man needs to feel connected to our Heavenly Father. With God, we know we can do all things. We know we can make it. At times, I found myself desperate and in need of more of God. I could not get enough of Him. I was invited to a women's Bible study. While I was there, a minister gave me a prayer line telephone number, and I'm grateful for it. I felt thirsty for a gentle touch from God. She sensed in the Spirit that I would appreciate it. I am so thankful for Mizpah Ministry because I needed so much prayer. I was becoming spiritually dehydrated. On the prayer line, there were people praying for me that had never seen me in person. The power of God's intercessors was pleading the blood of Jesus over my life, declaring that I would win and recover. This was what I needed - we all need it.

During the divorce process, we may need to get this I.V. pumping God's word into our spiritual veins. I needed my brain to stop racing. I am not trying to be religious, but

I am saying He who made you will order your footsteps. If you are seeking His face and knocking on the door, then it will be opened unto you.

> ✝ *O God, you are my God; Early will I seek You;*
> *My soul thirsts for You; My flesh longs for You*
> *In a dry and thirsty land Where there is no*
> *water.*
>
> Psalms 63:1

Often, when people go through difficulties, they do something to manage the pain. Retail shopping has been something I have often used. I love to find hidden treasures. You can easily find me at a thrift shop. Others turn to smoking cigarettes; some try to numb the pain with alcohol. There are some who will overeat day after day until their clothes stop fitting - they rearrange furniture or clean the whole house. I think everyone uses some type of coping skill to deal with an uncomfortable situation. In the past for other issues of life, I tried drinking. It never fixed anything. Instead of using other devices, I suggest getting hooked up to God's I.V. Do something that will profit your spirit. Avoid becoming dehydrated and stay in God's word.

> ✝ *As the deer pants longingly for the water brooks, so my soul pants longingly for You, O God. My soul my life, my inner self thirsts for God, for the living God. When will I come and see the face of God? My tears have been my food day and night, while they say to me all day long, "Where is your God?" These things I vividly remember as I pour out my soul; How I used to go along before the great crowd of people and lead them in procession to the house of God like a choir-master before his singers, timing the steps to the music and the chant of the song, With the voice of joy and thanksgiving, a great crowd keeping a festival. Why are you in despair, O my soul? And why have you become restless and disturbed within me? Hope in God and wait expectantly for Him, for I shall again praise Him for the help of His presence.*
>   Psalms 42:1-5

I started praying and studying God's word more. When the church doors opened on Sunday, I was there. At the end of the preached word, I went to altar. I watched and listened to great ministries on all my devices. You name it, my iPad, cell phone, DVR, DVD. I read over my spiritual journals. I wrote in my journal all prophetic and "Rhema" words (Greek for "spoken word). I needed the promises of God to stand on.

There are so many great ministries out there. Ministries have made their messages available to view twenty-four hours a day. These will equip you with the Word allowing you to feel the moving of the Holy Spirit. Yes, you can feel God's presence online, on the radio, and on the pages of books.

I needed the intimacy of the Father. All kind of questions were on my mind, "What Lord, what am I supposed to get out of the season?" After I had been putting my trust and hope in man or in idols, God was perfecting His Word in me. He wanted me to seek His face and look for Him and His directions. The same God wants to be found by each one of us. He wants us to thirst and crave hearing His voice. He wants to seek His will for our life. It pleases God when His children look to Him.

> ✝ *I love those who love me, and those who seek me diligently will find me.*
>
> Proverbs 8:17

Parents, you know what it's like to leave your small child for the day. When you return, the moment you enter, they drop everything and run to you. Even pet owners have seen how happy their animals get when they smell you near or hear the key in the lock. God wants us to do the same thing.

> ✝ *And they commanded the people, "When you see the ark of the covenant of the Lord your God being carried by the Levitical priests, then you shall set out from where you are and follow it. However, there shall be a distance between you and it of about*

> *2,000 cubits 3,000 ft. by measurement. Do not come near it, so that you may be able to see the ark and know the way you are to go, for you have not passed this way before.*
>
> Joshua 3:3-4

God is building you and your relationship with him. Follow His movement in the dark when your eyes can not see past the pain. In the drought, look for God to water you. In this process, He is also sharpening your hearing. He wants you to be able to recognize when the Holy Spirit is trying to comfort you.

It is vital that you hear that still, small voice of God and decipher when what you are hearing is from God and when it's NOT His voice. Sometimes we operate in err and we are being led by our emotions. Emotions, at times, sway from happy to sad. Therefore, they cannot be trusted to do what is right. They will cause us to do what satisfies the flesh in that moment. The flesh, if not under subjection will operate in a self-serving manner. In that state, emotions bring no benefits to others nor to the glory of God.

The voice of God can bring clarity and harmony to any situation. It allows love to be the punctuation at the end of the sentence. The voice of God provokes peace and righteousness. It causes us to be objective, not judgmental. It demands we see truth and not to believe the obvious lie. Hearing the voice of God has me looking for good. It doesn't leave me feeling anxious but, safe and confident that peace will be the outcome.

I pray that in the process, you won't get lost on your way to your breakthrough. This is a time for you to learn how to get the distractions out of your life; how to ignore the insignificant things. Staying focused will surely make you be the best version of yourself if you hold it together and submit to His voice of peace and love. Jesus is making intercession for you. You can scream that you are in pain, but afterward get relief from the Word of God.

Practical Application

1. Read the Word of God. Listen to the audio version of the Word of God.
2. You can watch great ministry on YouTube. Plenty of great ministries offer re-broadcasts of their services. There are thousands of amazing ministries, so find one to which you can relate.
3. Start a spiritual journal. Write down key parts of messages that encourage you. This is how we hear the voice of God.

Readers, let's go to prayer together.

Lord, I thank you for being with me, for giving me your wisdom and knowledge. Father, I ask that you help me in every area where I am weak and broken. Bring healing to me. Help me recover. Let your peace flow to every area of my life where there is confusion. In Jesus' Holy name, Amen.

✝

Declaration

I have a river of life flowing out of me.

Manifesto

I stand complete in Godly knowledge.

Music

Song: "I Will Trust"
Artist: Fred Hammond
Album: *I Will Trust*, 2014
Awards: Soul Train Music Award

Song: "I Won't Go Back"
Artist: William McDowell
Album: *Arise*, 2011

A LITTLE CHAT WITH A BIG GOD

Postscript to Chapter 4

I guess you can say I've been running. Running away from what I know I'm supposed to be doing. Feeling like our relationship was good, Lord. That you knew I loved you. But now I'm asking you to take complete control. Today I'm saying I surrender all to you. Revive me, restore me, and redeem me. I dedicate my life to you. I make you my Lord, my God, my Savior. Fill me up with the Holy Spirit. I want the mind of Christ Jesus – a sound mind. Forgive me for all of my mistakes, all of my wrongdoings. Transform me now, Lord. Use me for your glory. In Jesus' name, Amen.

CHAPTER 5

Firm Grip On You

In the scheme of things, our lifespan is short. With that in mind, every moment of life is valuable. There are times we must show tenacity and be persistent to achieve or possess what we want or desire. This is true in several areas of our life. We cannot be broad with what we want. It's best to specifically identify the object or situation we need or desire. When we apply for a job, we clearly specify which job we are applying for. Have you ever been at a restaurant and overheard someone placing an order? Sometimes they change their minds more than once until they are clear on what they want to order. The server usually gives them more time to decide. Likewise, when we are praying or believing God for something, He's waiting on us to decide, without wavering, what we want.

> ✝ *A double minded man is unstable in all his ways. God sees the indecisiveness and because you are unsure what you want. A little trust in God will help you figure out what you want.*
>
> James 1:8

Trusting God is not void of struggles. As for me, it has always paid off with great reward. I have never fallen on my face or looked like a fool. Even when I missed the original mark, things went favorable for me because of my trust in God. He will not turn His back on you. There is nothing so awful that He will cease to love you. Many things will change in your life. This will not be the only hard challenge you will ever go through. We are all students of life. We are continuously learning how to navigate with and acquire the skills to go to another level.

Expiration dates are on almost everything in life. For example, you could be a clerk for a couple of years. While you're in that position, you gain experience and knowledge. When a position with better pay and benefits comes along, you will be qualified to get that job. The previous job had expired, and it was time to move on. I believe that's how God's plans are for our lives. Treading on new territory and not know what the end is going to be can be frightening. Divorce papers can make you wonder, "What is going on?" "Who is looking out for me?"

When doors appear to be closing or is due to expire, trust God. He has something greater in store—and trust, you are capable and prepared for the next level. Even if you are single and not married, His loving plans are for you to live an abundant life. His plans for you are good – no, actually they are great. God has a firm grip on you, and nothing can snatch you out of his hands.

✝ *No weapon that is formed against you will succeed; And every tongue that rises against you in judgment you will condemn. This peace, righteousness, security, and triumph over opposition is the heritage of the servants of the Lord, and this is their vindication from Me, says the Lord.*
Isaiah 54:17

✝ *Behold, God will not reject a man of integrity, nor will He strengthen or support evildoers.*
Job 8:20

✝ *Keep your lives free from the love of money. Be happy with what you have. God has said, "I will never leave you or let you be alone." So, we can say for sure, "The Lord is my Helper. I am not afraid of anything man can do to me.*
Hebrews 13:5-6

✝ *The Lord will finish the work He started for me. O Lord, your loving-kindness lasts forever. Do not turn away from the works of Your hands.*
Jeremiah 29:11

✝ *You have never been tempted to sin in any different way than other people. God is faithful. He will not allow you to be tempted more than you can take. But when you are tempted, He will make a way for you to keep from falling into sin.*
1 Corinthians 10:13

Practical Application

1. Meditate on God's word and see yourself victorious. See yourself overcoming. See that God has a firm grip on you, and He is never letting you go.
2. There are several names for God. Take your time and explore them. Find a name of God that reminds you that you are His. A name that reminds you in this season of your life that God is directing you.
3. Do volunteer work for a nonprofit or help the less fortunate. This will help you emotionally feel good about yourself. It will also remind you how blessed you are.

Readers, let's go to prayer together.

Father, thank you for not abandoning me. Thank you for giving me strength. Lord, open my eyes, so I can always see that you are with me. Help me to trust you where I have doubt. Complete the work you started in me, God. Perfect those things that are concerning me. In Jesus' name, Amen.

Declaration

God has a firm grip on me; my life is safe.

Manifesto

I am kicking down doors and seizing my blessings.

Music

Song: "Breathe (This is the Air)"
Artist: Michael W. Smith
Album: Worship, 2001
Awards: Multiple Grammy Awards

Song: "Praise is What I Do"
Artist: Shekinah Glory and William McDowell
Album: *Praise is What I Do*, 2000

A LITTLE CHAT WITH A BIG GOD

Postscript to Chapter 5

I have been viewing my life from a broken lens; my focus is off. I'm standing in my truth right now. I want to be loved by you, to be kept safe by you. Remove the fog of insecurity and uncertainty, Lord. I've been looking for you my whole life. Lord, touch my life. I take you as my Father, my God. I believe in the great works of Jesus and the cross. Forgive my past and make me new. In Jesus' name, Amen.

CHAPTER 6

Whose Am I?

On television, I see people having divorce parties. They are celebrating the demise of their marriage. Some may feel, "I am so glad that it's over." Others wear a brave face like the breakup wasn't a big deal, or they carry on as if it is just another day. Then, there are those who get stuck in the past. Finally, we have the ones living in denial.

The morning after my spouse moved out of our home was surreal. When I went to the mailbox and found the final divorce papers in the mail, that moment delivered unspeakable emotions. My life was about to experience changes that would make me ask, "Whose am I?"

The business of divorce and changing documents to reflect single, changing my social media status to single were on my list of changes. Next, I had to go into the human resources office at work to update my paperwork. This included changing my emergency contact and medical insurance. I spent more hours changing my status than one could ever imagine. I remember contacting my life insurance company and all the credit card companies. Just when I thought I had called every company and made all the changes, some forgotten bank called me and asked for Mrs… I took a deep breath and slowly wiped the tears away because that was no longer me.

The divorce had been final for at least six months when I received a baby shower invitation addressing me as Mrs. I did not need the unwanted attention since there would be people there who would be learning about my situation for the first time. I also did not want to take attention away from the host. After all, it was her first baby shower.

I have heard people say that it's your friends who turn their backs on you when you transition from married to single. There's the issue of exclusion; not being invited to events because you are divorced. They treat you like you are a leper with rancid lesions all over your face. Some churchy, judgmental folks treat you like your divorced status means you have suddenly become a harlot. Now, you want everyone else's man when in fact, the newly single person is often prey for predators. Suddenly, coupled friends do not know how to interact with you because you have the "single" disease. Say bye-bye, to couple friends. You are single again.

Starting over is hard enough without trying to figure out why people you looked to as friends have suddenly disappeared. To them I say farewell! God bless you. It is said, "You learn who your friends are in hard times." Believe me, God is too good and merciful to worry about dinner invitations.

What about the question, "Are you ready to get back out there?" I talked "a really big game" during my separation. Silly stuff flowed from my mouth concerning future dating and what that life would look like. I said those things because I was mad and hurt. I even had someone send me a message about choosing your spouse. It was meant as a joke, but my divorce had been too soon for it to make me laugh. For me, the answer was, "no." I was not ready to get back out there. I needed to make sure I had both feet on the ground before meeting a potential someone. Texting, swiping to the left, and meeting people online wasn't a consideration either. It was my belief that when I was ready, God would send my spouse. Immediately following a divorce is the perfect season for us newly single people to fall in love with self and discover how fabulous we are. To see ourselves created by God.

I just described how the business world, friends and family see you. Do you know who you are? In Louisiana, Creole people ask, "Who you for?" which means, "Who is your family?" As a married person, that was an easy question to answer. Let me say it for you. You belong to God, even if you remarry, and I sincerely hope you do. God made you. He always loved you. He never wants you to be separated from Him. You belong to God; you are for Him.

It is God who keeps you. He took your feet out of the slop and the stinky. He cleaned you up and will never let you go. His grace keeps you. You belong to Him. God is so into you. He created you in His image. Nothing about you was accidental. He took His time creating you as His masterpiece.

> ✝ *Then God said, "Let Us Father, Son, Holy Spirit make man in Our image, according to Our likeness not physical, but a spiritual personality and moral likeness; and let them have complete authority over the fish of the sea, the birds of the air, the cattle, and over the entire earth, and over everything that creeps and crawls on the earth." So God created man in His own image, in the image and likeness of God He created him; male and female He created them.*
> *Genesis 1:26-27*

✝ *When I see and consider Your heavens, the work of Your fingers, the moon and the stars, which You have established, what is man that You are mindful of him, And the son of earthborn man that You care for him? Yet You have made him a little lower than God, And You have crowned him with glory and honor. You made him to have dominion over the works of Your hands; You have put all things under His feet.*

Psalms 8:3-6

✝ *You made all the delicate, inner parts of my body and knit them together in my mother's womb. Thank you for making me so wonderfully complex! It is amazing to think about. Your workmanship is marvelous—and how well I know it. You were there while I was being formed in utter seclusion! You saw me before I was born and scheduled each day of my life before I began to breathe. Every day was recorded in your book! How precious it is, Lord, to realize that you are thinking about me constantly! I can't even count how many times a day your thoughts turn toward me. And when I waken in the morning, you are still thinking of me! Yes, I hate them, for your enemies are my enemies too.*

Psalms 139:13-17, 22

If your children, mother, or best friend don't call to check on you daily, it's okay. Your God is always thinking about you. When you are asleep, snoring and dreaming, God is still thinking about you. He is the lover of your soul. He loves you with an everlasting love. God's love is not based on something you did or said. No merits, no performance, nothing you have done can make Him sway His decision.

God loves you, husband or not, wife or not. Others may never appreciate you, but His love is sufficient. God calls you His special and chosen child. He crowned you with glory and honor. He is proud of you. He has always had a plan for your life. He placed His faith inside of you; His spirit inside of you. [See 1 Peter 2:9, Psalms 8:5].

God numbered the hairs on your head. If you picked a hand full of hair from your head right now and lifted a few strands up, He could say that is number 13 and 70 she is holding. In the same token, He knows all the details of your life.

God created you to win. No matter what challenges came with your divorce, regardless of who left you or who talked about you. God has only great thoughts of you. It doesn't matter how you may have messed up; God is still on your side. He still claims you as His child, His beloved. [See 2 Corinthians 6:18].

Whose am I? You are an heir of God, joint heir of heavenly things. Put your shoulders back and lift your head up. Look people in their eyes. Get your confidence up because you're extraordinary. Through God you are not defeated. Yes, in divorce there is confusion and there may be feelings of despair. Those feelings are temporary. Stay strong. You are the heir of God.

> ✝ *And lifted us up from the grave into glory along with Christ, where we sit with Him in the heavenly realms—all because of what Christ Jesus did.*
> Ephesians 2:6

> ✝ *And if children, then heirs; heirs of God, and joint-heirs with Christ; if so be that we suffer with Him, that we may be also glorified together.*
> Romans 8:17

HE HAS YOUR NAME ENGRAVED IN THE PALM OF HIS HAND

What God is saying is, "You for me!" I love you so much that I have a portrait of you tattooed unto the palm of my hand. Every time He opens His hands, He sees you. God is always thinking about you, His beloved child. You are always in His sight. You may have taken your wedding ring off, but God did not take you off His mind. Your father in heaven carries you, not close, not just near Him, but carries you with Him.

> ✝ *Can a woman forget her nursing child, And not have compassion on the son of her womb? Surely they may forget, Yet I will not forget you. See, I have inscribed you on the palms of My hands; Your walls are continually before Me.*
>
> Isaiah 49:15-16

You were created for a purpose. God is carrying you through the tough times. He will not let depression or grief take you from Him. Nothing that the devil tries will snatch you out of your Heavenly Father's hands. He knows how to bring you back from this divorce. He can and will restore you. God has doors He will open for you because you are His and you are highly favored. The favor of God rests on your life. Which is why it is so important for you to keep your faith in God strong. Keep building yourself up by relying on His Word. See yourself as highly favored by God.

When Roman kings wrote letters or decrees, they would put stamps on the documents. They were engraved specifically for each king. The seal represented the authorization, authentication, and the power of the king who was backing and enforcing the letter. God has given that same power to you. You have been sealed by God. He sealed you with His favor and protection. Everywhere you go, realize that you have the seal of favor on your life.

God delights in you. He has set you apart for all to see you belong to Him. If you delight yourself in God, He will delight Himself in you. To have continued favor of God, it's important to live a life pleasing to Him. It is your reasonable service. Change your perspective on how you see yourself. Speak out of your mouth what God says about you. It makes me sad to see believers not knowing or realizing how special they are to God. This is a key part of your life. I watch people get lost and begin to do life without God, and they struggle so hard, repeatedly getting hit. Your faith is influenced by your thoughts and confessions. A life with God requires believing that every promise in the Bible is yours. It is with faith you will obtain it.

> ✝ *For we are His workmanship, created in Christ Jesus for good works, which God prepared beforehand that we should walk in them.*
> Ephesians 2:10

YOU ARE THE RIGHTEOUSNESS OF GOD

> ✝ *As for you, you were dead in your transgressions and sins, But because of His great love for us, God, who is rich in mercy, made us alive with Christ even when we were dead in transgressions—it is by grace you have been saved. And God raised us up with Christ and seated us with Him in the heavenly realms in Christ Jesus, in order that in the coming ages he might show the incomparable riches of His grace, expressed in His kindness to us in*

> *Christ Jesus. For it is by grace you have been saved, through faith—and this is not from your-selves, it is the gift of God.*
>
> Ephesians 2:1, 4-8

Being a child of God doesn't mean you will not go through tough times, difficulties, and (dare I say) divorce. It does not make you exempt from calamity. It makes you have His support, His protection, His hand upon you. Mary was highly favored and blessed to birth Jesus. She and Joseph still had to run and hide. She had our Savior in a barn with animals surrounding her. Then there was Jacob's son, Joseph in the Old Testament. Jacob loved him and gave him a coat of many colors that represented his favor. He spent days in a pit, was sold into slavery, and went to prison. Yet God had a plan for his life. Despite the many obstacles Joseph faced, the visions and dreams God promised him still came to pass. Hold on to the promise of God. He has chosen you. You belong to God. You are His son or daughter, and our Lord has great and mighty things planned for your life. The best is yet to come.

Child of God, getting through divorce with faith is the only way. Continuously hear the Word of God. Hear it, believe it, and receive the promises. That is how you will find out all the benefits that come with His grace. This is how you come out on the other side of divorce victoriously. Your days of pain will be shorter when you recognize that His favor, blessing, good deeds, kindness, special provision, health, welfare, peace, and joy are surrounding you. This is how He shows up for those who are for Him.

Practical Application

Write out some of the promises of God and say them daily. There are so many products like calendars and books with the promise of God – pick one up. Remind yourself of His promises in any way you can because He is the only one who will never break a promise.

Readers, let's go to prayer together.

Lord God, I thank you for giving me revelation on who you made me to be. I thank you, God, that you have equipped me with everything I need to be successful in life. Lord, shower me with your love. Continue to open the eyes of my understanding. In Jesus' powerful name, Amen.

Declaration

I am God's favorite child.

Manifesto

I will leave my footprint on this earth
being exactly what God made me.

Music

Song: "I Am"
Artist: Jason Nelson
Album: *Jesus Revealed*, 2015
Awards: Stellar Award

A LITTLE CHAT WITH A BIG GOD

Postscript to Chapter 6

Today I am looking over my life, and it looks like it's not heading in the direction I had wanted. I try, but I fall down. I make so many mistakes. Sometimes I feel so overwhelmed, thinking what's the point?

So, I want a relationship with you, Lord. I want you to forgive me of my sins. I want you to take these burdens away from me. I make you my God today, my Lord and Savior. I believe in you that you're the only one who can help me in life. I ask you to have free reign over me. Fill me up with your love. Fill me with your power, your strength. I receive all that you have for me today. In Jesus' name, Amen.

CHAPTER 7

My Identity Is In God

The reality is I have come to understand that my ex-husband and I were brought into each other's lives for a reason, but I am not sure if it was for marriage... We were from two different worlds. I wanted him to live up to my standards and he wanted me to live like him. One day, I was soul searching and asked myself, "How did I marry someone so different?" I surmised that my head was not clear. I was going through a transitional period. Being that I was not focused, I was filled with self-doubt and my self-image was fractured compromise took up residence. Suzánne was not standing as the strong and powerful person that God created her to be. In essence, I made a permanent decision based on my temporary emotional status.

When I was at a low point in my life, this man walked in like a knight in shining armor. Unfortunately, the story didn't end like a Cinderella story. I did not get married because I wanted a wedding day. I wasn't looking to wear the fancy dress or have an audience of onlookers. What I was longing for was family. Not only was I marrying him, but I would also be gaining, daughters, a mother-in-law, aunts, siblings, and nieces that I had previously cultivated a relationship with. The family showed me love and treated me as if I was theirs.

My ex-husband came with a family big enough to fill the hole inside me. The grand matriarch of the family, his aunt loved me. She spent nights at my home. I did her hair and took her to doctor's appointments. Most of all, she enjoyed my cooking. She once told me that I reminded her of herself … exactly the thing a mother would say. I latched on to that, not because I was eager to get married. I wasn't a woman who was desperate for marriage, but I was desperate for family.

Blinded by my need for family, I didn't acknowledge any red flags. One day, my prince walked into the room and all of his armor fell to the ground. The real him was beginning to surface. I asked God before I married him, if he was the one. He never said no but then again, He never said yes either. That's why God said he wanted to heal me from the past hurts. It is so important to grieve properly and not to just cover it up.

Mirror, mirror on the wall
My identity had slipped to a fall
I accepted less than I deserved
Created a mess from my emotions
I was trying to build a family
That is what I longed for
Losing you, Mom left a hole
That I could not fill
Only the greatest love
could stimulate my heart
…to beat without a murmur
Lord, save me

by Suzánne Eaglin

My mom, Gloria passed away when I was 20 years old and pregnant. Mom had promised that she would help me with the baby. Now that she was gone, I had no one. My relationship with my biological father was uncommon. He was not a mainstay in my life. My stepdad was supposed to adopt me, but never did. That left me fragmented and wondering why. I knew beyond a shadow of a doubt that my granddad loved me. Unfortunately, he'd passed away one year before my mom did.

I believe that parents recognize and nurture their child's lives and dreams. Lacking that in my life made it hard for me to develop a positive self-image. It also distorted how I valued myself. Whenever I had life challenges, the hole grew bigger. I constantly sought validation. I'd ask myself, "Was I a good daughter, mother, sister, even a good granddaughter?" Life brought rejections, disappointments, and more grief. Being a single parent was no easy task. Many days I found myself wishing I could get advice from my mom.

I lived several states away from my biological family members. For years, I created a family of my own. It consisted of friends that I had adopted into my life and heart. Over thirty years ago in ninth grade, I met one of my best friends. We've shared life's victories, challenges, births, deaths and everything in between. My mom was like a mother figure to her. At my wedding, her mom walked down the aisle and stood in place of my mom since my mom is deceased. My friend and I even lived together at one time. Like sisters, we have had our disagreements. Even though we have grown up, have children and grand babies of our own, we still consider ourselves as family.

During the year my son was graduating high school, I was buying a house and recovering from shoulder surgery. That's when Prince Charming entered, stage left.

In the midst of me buying my home, at one point it fell out of escrow. It appeared as if I was not going to fulfill the American dream. He was there, encouraging me and also assisted me financially. Shortly after my shoulder surgery, clumps of my hair started falling out, resulting in several bald spots.

The pain of the surgery and the hair loss caused me to slip into a depression, but he was right there telling me how beautiful I was. For my son's prom, he offered to buy his suit. We stood side by side at my son's graduation. He was careful to remind me although my son's father was absent from his life, I still held it down.

My father's taught me how to love. Growing up, I was blessed to have three dads. My biological dad showed up when I was visiting my grandmother in Louisiana. He was the fun dad who took me shopping. Growing up, I knew my stepdad as daddy. He was a Vietnam Navy veteran. He suffered from post-traumatic stress disorder and a brain injury. There were days he could talk to me, then there were periods where he would not.

He was my protector and provider. Every boy interested in me had to go through him. The challenge I had with him is that he did not deal with issues as it related to his injuries. This taught me to ignore my personal challenges. This would prove to be a continued issue in my life. My grandfather loved me from the day I was born until the day he died. He referred to me as his angel. I was privileged to be his first grandchild and honored to have his last name.

> *"Don't you fall now --*
> *For I'se still goin', honey,*
> *I'se still climbin',*
> *Life ain't been no Crystal Stairs"*
>
> "Mother to Son"
> by Langston Hughes

"If"
by Rudyard Kipling

If you can meet with Triumph and Disaster
And treat those two impostors just the same;
If you can bear to hear the truth you've spoken
Twisted by knaves to make a trap for fools,
Or watch the things you gave your life to, broken,
And stoop and build 'em up with worn-out tools:

Although I was broken, cracked and chipped from afflictions, I was safely healed by God's hand. My mom had done her job. She raised me to be the woman I am today. I am strong, tenacious and courageous. I have a powerful voice. The words I speak come from a place of love. I use my words to heal the broken. God peeled back the layers. He opened my shell where the precious jewels hide. I am a God made treasure.

Your Imagine

A positive self-image is important to end an identity crisis. There are no limits except the ones you put on yourself. You have a creative force inside you. Belief in yourself is the energy you need to stop being miserable. You have to expand your way of thinking of who you are. How you see yourself will either cause you to live unbreakable or shatter at the blow of wind. You have to become the person you have been made by God to be. All of your experience will help define yourself. Think about the difficult times in your life. How did they define you? What step will you take in incorporating what you learn into perfecting your identity.

What drives me comes from the challenges of losing my mother. I have compassion and want to help young mothers and single parents. I also help young ladies growing up with a single mom. I can identify with the struggle and the need for a village to surround them. Instead of allowing the challenges to be a hindrance or keep me off balance, I've found my voice. I give aid to the hurting.

I did not consider what I had. I only thought about what I didn't have. In my mind the loss of my mom was greater than what I possessed. The mind is a beautiful place. It holds all your consciousness, unconscious patterns, your mental activities, reasoning, feelings and judgment. Our mind is very powerful. Think about what you have gained from what you have lived through and make those encounters beneficial. Your identity cannot be based on the amount of money you have or material things. What you have is greater than money. Your identity is powerful and profitable.

Response to God

We have to expand our way of thinking. God created us. We are all His children. No matter what human imperfections we have, regardless if you made mistakes, we can still identify ourselves as God's beloved child. God showed me by prayer and meditation how to identify my identity.

Do Nots

Do not allow negative things you have heard from your past to hinder you from believing in yourself. Do not push away or deny feeling good or your new value. It takes courage to pick yourself back up from a fall. It's okay to give yourself a high-five for your accomplishments. Society will bring you lots of images for you to identify with. Strong emotional stamina will keep you motivated to operate in your full potential. Remove all toxic thoughts about you and mistakes you have made. This is self-destructive and you are causing yourself harm. This way of thinking is destroying you from the inside out. Keep in mind we are all not perfect people. We are all flawed and make many mistakes. Learn what not to do from those scenarios. The things you continue to beat yourself up about, if someone you loved was in your situation, would you have compassion for them? Would you show empathy for others and use kind words to help encourage them? Then, get a mirror out and encourage yourself. Treat yourself with love, admiration and respect. How you treat yourself will create the guide for how others will treat you.

Readers, let's again pray together.

Thank you, Lord, for making me and proudly claiming me as your child. I thank you today that the blood of Jesus covers and protects me. Bless my life each and every day. Let your anointing guide me to walk in my purpose. I rest in you. In Jesus' name, Amen.

Declaration

I walk with the confidence of God.

Manifesto

I am rocking the runway of my life walking in my purpose.

Music

Song: "I'm Yours"
Artist: Casey J
Album: *The Truth*, 2015
Awards: GMA Dove Award Nominee

Song: "All I Have to Give"
Artist: Mali
Album: *The Second Coming*, 2011
Awards: GMA Dove Award

A LITTLE CHAT WITH A BIG GOD

Postscript to Chapter 7

Up until this moment in my life, I have not believed in much. I have believed that everything has little to no meaning, but I want more. I've heard that you are a God of plenty, of abundance. I want the abundant life. So today I acknowledge that you are God, that you are Lord. You died on the cross for my sins. You have forgiven me. Thank you for forgiving me. Come into my life and fill me with all the promises of your words. I want to live differently. I want the best life I can have. So be my Lord and direct me, so I can live to glorify you and be my most authentic self. I want to live knowing I am yours. In Jesus' name, Amen.

CHAPTER 8

Where Is My Cheer Team?

One thing that can help you get through the divorce process easier, is if you have at least one ride or die friend. That friend who will stick to you and check on you when you try to disappear from the world. This friend is not moved by your shortcomings. What do I mean? A friend who will not judge or be critical of you. This friend will not kick you while you are hurting. God speaks very highly of friendships in the Bible. *"One who has unreliable friends soon comes to ruin, but there is a friend who sticks closer than a brother"* (Proverbs 18:24 NIV).

If I have a moment of fussing, complaining or saying things that are out of character, I need my friend to understand. If I'm emotional, crying my eyes out, I may need my friend to just listen. Everyone needs a friend they can vent to - the friend who can help you transition a negative mood to a pleasant disposition.

As previously mentioned, your acquaintances and friendship circles seem to change during divorce. Some people will shift, transform, or even remove themselves from you. I learned firsthand; in the hard times you will learn who these people really are.

In this season, concentrate on new value systems. It's important to surround yourself with people who share your same values. Focus on transforming yourself from the inside out. Your new team can act as a mirror and reflect positive situations. Goal setting will destroy negativity that is trying to invade your world as well. You cannot be victorious if you are stagnant. Identify the team members who will be vital in your growth

Your team is comprised of the company you keep. If you find yourself friendless, pray to the Father to send you one. He knows exactly who and what you need. I have a friend who has never been married. The changes she was making in her life were like the changes I was making after my divorce. Having mutual life goals and common ground is a key factor in friendship. Good friends can be great for growth. The wrong friends can stunt your growth. Please avoid negative influences.

The Gossipers

Gossipers are ready to talk about someone. If you want that type of person in your life, know that they most likely will gossip about you too. The gossiper's life is spent finding fault, blaming, and being jealous of other people. [See Proverbs 6:16-19]. Do you want a friend like that? You might want to avoid that gossiping bunch of people. Continuous victories cannot be won if your circle's foundation is shaky. Opportunities will be missed when you should be advancing your life forward.

The Complainers

Complainers are a bunch of people who have an excuse for everything. These are people who will steal your confidence right out of your heart. They are a griping natured people who do not have anything because of all the unfair breaks they have experienced. Guess what?

They are not a fan of you rising and breaking glass ceilings that stand in your way of going higher in advancement. They like their group to be filled with negative words and huge lackadaisical speeches. You begin to speak and share something that is happening in your life, and they will tell a story of their own that is twenty times worse. They have been there in the dark for a very long time. In fact, they live there in "Oh it is poor old me land." They have been there so long they do not know which way "fulfillment" went. I know you know them. We all know people like this. When you ask, "What are you doing today?" And every response is continuous sad talk and pity. [See Philippians 2:14].

The Procrastinators

Procrastinators are the 'should have', 'would have', 'could have' people. Often, they have the ability and the know-how. However, because they put-off and delay action, nothing ever gets done. They lack organizational skills and seldom prioritize what's important. They live on the fly—absent from an appointment book. They fly by the seat of their pants. The procrastinator is the next "great success." Due to procrastination, the world may never know their names. They miss opportunities that were perfect for them because they succumbed and became their own distractions. [See Ecclesiastes 11:3-4 and Proverbs 6:4].

The Compromisers

Compromisers are perfectly content with their lives. They are satisfied with the same routine. They drive the same car, and they require no upgrades. They have more knowledge than most on the job. In some cases, they have trained others. They should be managers, but instead they are content being a subordinate. Good people often operate in pure complacency. They could launch their own business. Often, they are naturally talented and highly gifted. Too bad they are okay with receiving that check that comes once a month. They will see something nice that sparks their interest but will pass on it. They have an "if it's not broke don't fix it mentality." You will not see them work hard to get what they want. They do not stretch their thoughts beyond the basic. The compromiser stays in the frame. They don't think out of the box. [See Ephesians 5:15-17 and Proverbs 12:24].

The Dream Killers

Dream killers are like walking fly swatters. This person will beat someone else's dream down. If you say, "I am about to go to college," Their response is, "It's so expensive, where are you going to get the money? You really think you're cut out for college?" These people will hear your dreams and make you question your own ambition. Can I do this? Is it too big for me? Is it too much to ask for? You have just been around a dream killer. You visit them feeling good and high on life, having an amazing day. You go over for a quick visit. Then you accidentally spend fifteen minutes too long and leave feeling heavy and sad. You have just been with a dream killer. Their presence is like a statue. It dominates the room. My suggestion when you meet a dream killer is run in the other direction!

It is our responsibility to cultivate a healthy, supportive environment. If negative actions or responses of others prevent us from being who we want to be, it is up to us to remove them. Your life is your own. Every decision belongs to you. People can inspire you to greatness or toward destruction.

Where is my cheer team? My cheer team can be found uplifting my spirit. I can call them to let some steam off. By the end of a conversation, I will be left feeling good, safe and cracking up in laughter.

A cheer team is comprised of those who will rally around you. They give you sincere accolades on your success. By definition, a cheer team yells out encouraging words. They can openly say positive things about your accomplishments. They believe in you. They are not threatened by you because they are for you. If I mention to my team that I am going back to college for my degree. Their reply is "That is wonderful. That is good. I believe in you. You can do it!"

Squad

The dictionary definition is, *"a small number of soldiers assembled for drill or assignments to special task, especially an infantry unit forming a part of a platoon."*

My squad is a phenomenal, hand-selected small group of people I associate and go to events with. This team is also comprised of people who tend to be activists. This strong group of women head companies and non-profit organizations. Some of my squad does volunteer work in the community. If one of us is successful in an area, the knowledge is passed on so that we all glean information. We reach down and pull each other up to a higher plain to motivate, network and inspire others. We seek knowledge to be better people. When we are in formation, we make a positive impact to improve everything around us.

I have heard people say, "I don't need anybody." In relationships, there will be disappointments. Please be careful not to become a victim and become discouraged. It's not fair to your squad if you have not shared what support you need in the season. Keep communication lines open and honest. My friends have told me, "I am here for you for whatever you need. You want me to drive the getaway car? You need me to have a quick chat with someone? Need me to bring you some food or take you out for dinner? Should I go with you to turn in the divorce papers? I got you at whatever state your life is in, I got your back."

† *...And one standing alone can be attacked and defeated, but two can stand back-to-back and conquer; three is even better, for a triple-braided cord is not easily broken.*
Ecclesiastes 4:12

Leaning on a Friend

Sometimes you will experience a level of pain in your heart that makes you barely able to speak. It is during those times you may want to be able to call a friend and cry. They answer the telephone, hear your condition, and just start praying for you. This friend calls you in the middle of the night saying, "You were just so heavy on my heart and mind." God will give you what you need in a friend. Philippians 4:19: says, *"...And my God shall supply all your need according to His riches in glory by Christ Jesus. Walking in life with a true friend in my opinion is a basic need."* God said it is not good for man to walk alone. Whether you are married or not, relationships with other people are necessary and important.

Surround yourself with positive, goal-driven people; this will make a long day seem easier. If your friendships are bringing value, keep them; if they are not, delete, delete, delete. I want a friend who will be in the trenches with me. I'd like a friend who will fast and pray with and for me. When I am discouraged, they can go to God for me. This is the friend that will rebuke the devil on my behalf. A friend will stick close to you and fight for you when you're weary. You need someone who will protect you when you are not even around. They will not let someone speak badly about you.

> ✝ *A friend loves at all times, and a brother is born for adversity.*
> Proverbs 17:17

We choose our friends but not our family. There are times, we want our biological family to love and support us. Just because they are family doesn't mean we can depend on them. If you find a friend who sticks as close to you as a brother, I encourage you to be grateful and receive them. [See Proverbs 27:10].

> ✝ *Can two walk together, unless they are agreed?*
> Amos 3:3

For example, you and I are friends. We are taking a walk to the gym together. We meet up and decide to go a specific route. We agreed to walk down Atlantic towards Willow street. If you go left, and I go right, we are not in agreement. We must agree on which path to take.

> ✝ *Now when he had finished speaking to Saul, the soul of Jonathan was knit to the soul of David, and Jonathan loved him as his own soul. Saul took him that day and would not let him go home to his father's house anymore. Then Jonathan and David made a covenant, because he loved him as his own soul. And Jonathan took off the robe that was on him and gave it to David, with his armor, belt.*
>
> 1 Samuel 18:5

For example, the friendship of David and Jonathan was the result of divine grace. It produces in true believers one heart and one soul – or true friends who love each other. This union of souls is from partaking in the Spirit of Christ. This is a place where God unites hearts; carnal matters are too weak to separate them. Those who love Christ as their own souls will be willing to join themselves to Him in an everlasting covenant.

Smart Devices and Moments

I recall being invited to a barbecue during the summer. There were about eight of us. I went to the restroom. Upon my return, I saw everyone was looking at their phones. It is important to create moments with the people you associate with. Value the time you spend with your friends.

People's time is far too valuable for you to take it for granted. Laugh with people. Look at them in their faces. Do you know what they were wearing? Turn everything off and be in the moment with your friend. Be connected with your community. [See Ruth 1:16].

Social media postings are not a reliable source. If they are not reaching out, they may be silently telling you, they are hurting. Sometimes, you can tell just by hearing your friend's voice how they are doing. Pick up the phone or drop by for a visit and check on them regularly.

Truth, authenticity, understanding, and intentionality that is what it takes to sustain good friendships. A real ride or die friend should be able to speak into all the areas of your life. Those the public see and those behind closed doors. We need someone to be able to tell us the truth about us even when we do not want to hear it. Doing this helps us to grow. Superficial friendships are built on lies, fakeness, and coincidence.

When my friends saw me fall into the pit of divorce, they came with love ropes ready to pull me out of depression. At times, they saw my faith slipping. They held my hand and prayed for me. When all I could do was cry, I had a friend listen to every murmur and whimper, as she held the box of Kleenex. "Let's go do something for a few hours to get your mind off things."

During the season of rebuilding my life I had a cheer team saying, "Yes, girl, you got this. You buried your mom and raised a male child as a single parent. You have experienced worse; this will not kill you. You got what it takes to survive."

I saw a portrait of lions walking. I believe the caption read, "You're on your mission, your grind in life, and you need to walk with others who are on a mission." As I looked at the picture, many inspirational thoughts came to mind. Surround yourself with people who are strong-minded and full of positivity. It made me think of eagles; I associate with people who fly above mountains of obstacles to soar over giant issues. I want to go places chickens cannot imagine because their wings will not take them. I will fly to live an abundant life but cannot do it hanging with the hens.

I had to say goodbye to people to folks who reminded me of negative stuff during that season of divorce. I was not going to let my divorce make me a cynical person. Their intention was to get me to question everything. I didn't need to be criticized to the point where I would feel like, "dung." That perspective was not helpful to me. I used to brag on my marriage, my love for my husband. There were those who tried me, who came for me with harsh jokes that hurt me. [See Ephesians 5:4].

Accept the shift and move on...

Don't be surprised if you are left out or don't get what you need at church. Married people and singles do not understand what divorce people need. Divorced people need a support system not a social club. Invitations rolled in immediately when you got married, however with one announcement of divorce, the invitations dry up. This happened long before my divorce papers had even been filed. It didn't matter about the friendships I thought I'd cultivated. I had to pull out my compact mirror just to look for the scarlet letter. Did I stop being a person of good and kind-hearted intentions? Did I stop being the person who had been a true friend to them? Was I about to advise them to act single? Certainly not.

By nature, I am slow to anger, quick to forgive and give people several chances. At times, my divorce challenges brought out sarcasm and laughter in me. Someone who was very close to me told me "You are tripping too much over your breakup." She compared the length of her twenty-year marriage to my three-year marriage. My heartbreak and recovery were too emotional. To me, the implication was my heartache was not significant. I too stood in front of witnesses and before God and entered into holy wedlock. I believe it was based on the same love she felt for her husband. It was an unfair comparison. I thought, "Please stop talking to me. Remove yourself from me and sit down somewhere. Go have several seats in the Staple Center. My life will be victorious." A little distance from people in a season of divorce may happen and be necessary for you to heal properly.

Goodbye to people who could not show up for me. Goodbye to fair weather friends. Go join the audience of my life. Get a good seat. I must say goodbye to you, so I can live. I was in a storm, no visits, no telephone calls. Were you really a friend? Here is what I am saying, if you go to an NBA game, you sit amongst thousands. People are yelling good and bad things at the players and coach. The coach never looks up to them for the advice.

Do not share your life with people who do not love and celebrate you. I put distance between myself and those who are complaining, compromising, dream killing, procrastinating, and gossiping. If I was going to survive, I needed strong people to help me stay focused. Staying sane and coming out better was my focus during divorce.

You have permission to remove yourself from people who will stop you from becoming successful. Keep them in your prayers. Pray for them to live their best life. Accept the shift and move on. Own everything that is happening in your life. You make free choices every day. Do not include dysfunctional people. Save their visit for holidays and family reunions. Fight to keep your mind healthy.

Who you hang around is who you are most like. There is an old saying, "Show me who your friends are, and I will tell you who you are." In the process of changing your life, you have to seriously consider with whom you associate. Add people to your life who are living life large. Add people to your life who are successful and have accomplishments.

My favorite quote from Maya Angelou is this, "When someone shows you who they are the first time, believe them." I watch what people do. That's a better indicator on who they are. People will show you their truth. It is your job to believe it. Look for a person's action. Let it speak for their character.

Practical Application

1. Release negative friendships and be forgiving.
2. Figure out what type of friends you want in your life.
3. Identify the company you keep.
4. Communicate your expectations.
5. Friendship requires work. Be willing to do it.

Readers, it's time to pray together.

Lord Jesus, I need a friend. I am asking you to send me someone to be there for me through this process. Send someone that can motivate me to be my best self. Let them be gentle enough to be loving and caring. Lord, send me a friend with the love and commitment that David and Ruth had. Tear down any wall around my heart. Teach me to be a friend that would stick closer than a brother. In Jesus' name, Amen.

✝
Declaration

No longer oppressed but filled with the joy of the Lord.

Manifesto

I live in a circle of love

Music

Song: "Alpha and Omega"
Artist: Israel Houghton
Album: *Alive in South Africa*, 2005

Awards: Grammy Award
Song: "My Life is in Your Hands"
Artist: Kirk Franklin
Album: *God's Property*, 1997
Awards: Grammy Award

A LITTLE CHAT WITH A BIG GOD

Postscript to Chapter 8

I'm tired. Mentally exhausted. I've heard that you will help me, that you will protect me, that you will heal me. I want that assistance, that protection, that healing for myself. I've been told I can try Jesus. So today I will. Father God, I ask that you forgive my sins. Come into my life and give me your peace. I want everything that you have for me. I believe that you alone are God. I have made so many mistakes, done so many things that I am not proud of. Forgive me. Please. I believe that Jesus went to the cross so that I could be forgiven and made whole. I choose to walk with you today and every day for the rest of my life. Give me the life I was meant to live. In Jesus' name, Amen.

CHAPTER 9

Emergency Evacuation

Domestic abuse physically or mentally is terrible. I celebrate you if you've removed yourself from an abusive marriage. This is huge. Domestic violence has taken the lives of many women and men each year. Parents are their children's role models. They can influence their child for both good and bad. Children who see abuse grow up believing it must be normal behavior. There are many life-defining behaviors children living in domestic violent homes learn. First, the child can grow up and find themselves in an abusive relationship. The second common result is huge trust issues. They have difficulties being in loving, healthy relationships because they don't trust it. Third, hatred could set into their hearts. They build defensive walls to keep everyone out. Hatred could open them up to perverse sexual tendencies. It is not just girls, but boys as well. Abuse is not gender specific. Men are also abused. However, they tend to suffer in silence.

Abuse, no matter what kind or who the perpetrator is, is wrong. The victims are affected in ways that are unimaginable. Behind closed doors, there is often shouting, name-calling, belittling and more. The victim is made to feel like they cannot do anything right. Idiot is etched in one's mind because the abuser says they are. The perpetrator controls the victim's life. They must report in and are told what to do with most of their day. The recipient of abuse jumps hoops and walks tightropes to avoid any conflict. They do not want another explosive rage that generally comes from seemingly nowhere. Victims are bullied, intimidated, and live in constant fear. At some point, the abuser appears to feel remorse. Next comes fictitious adoration, a heartfelt sorry, and empty promises. One wrong word or movement and you could set them off to explode again. The alarm inside you says, "It is about to happen again."

Your home should be your sanctuary. It should not be a place of screams filled with terror and fear. As a young adult, I remember living next door to my aunt and uncle. One night my little cousins who were seven and five banged their little fists against our iron screen door. Their voices rang out into the night, "Help, help, come quick. My daddy is killing my mommy." My mother and I ran from our home wearing no shoes. I do not think we even stopped to close the door behind us. The sight of my uncle hitting my aunt was so scary to me. My aunt was not a small, frail woman. She was six feet, strong, and powerful. My uncle was just a little bit taller than her. They were on the floor in the hallway. He had his knees over her shoulder blades. He had her pinned down and was basically sitting on her. Her head and neck were between his knees. With one hand he was punching her. He took his other hand and had his fingers wrapped in her hair. He was using her hair to slam her head into the ground. His children were right if we would have been sleeping, she would have died that night. It took all the strength my mom and I had to get him off her. He was so out of control. He hit his own sister for interfering. I was next. He pushed me, and I was almost four months pregnant. I am not afraid of the boogie man in cartoons. I am afraid of domestic violence and the scary monsters people turn into.

My aunt divorced him and took the kids. My male cousin had so many problems after that. He has been sentenced to thirty years in jail at only eighteen. Once he and I spoke on the telephone. He said that horrible night changed him forever. He never got the therapy he needed. He was robbed of a childhood.

I asked a woman who had left an abusive marriage, what the hardest part was. Her reply was, "Learning to live without the abuse." Always second guessing yourself becomes second nature. This happens because the abuser has dominated you for so long. Now one must be reprogrammed to believe that he or she could be happy and free.

After bravely leaving an abusive situation one must learn new life skills. As stated earlier, many churches may have made you feel bad about your decision or that God was against the decision to divorce. However, God loves you and wants you to be healthy and have a life filled with His joy and peace. Abuse is not a punishment or a test from God.

Here are the side effects that a person who has been abused will suffer:

- No or low self-confidence
- Quiet
- Depression
- Withdrawal
- Low self-esteem
- Emotional instability
- Restless sleep
- Physical pain
- Suicidal thoughts or attempts
- Extreme dependence on the abuser

Does the Bible state clearly without any doubt that you should leave your marriage if you are being abused? The Bible does not in plain language make the statement that if you are being abused you are free to leave with God's blessings. The Bible says husbands are to love their wives as their own bodies. Just as Christ loved the church [See Ephesians 5:28–29].

In fact, over the years we have seen or heard of Christians staying in abusive marriages. They have been taught that it is God's will for their life to stay in an abusive marriage. I just described a very cruel God if that were true. It is not true not at all!

> ✝ *Wives, in the same way submit yourselves to your own husbands so that, if any of them do not believe the word, they may be won over without words by the behavior of their wives.*
> 1 Peter 3:1-2

Men and women alike have lost their lives from the hand of an abuser. Death has been the outcome of too many abusive marriages. Often, children are left dysfunctional. As a result, I know kids who hate God because their parent died in an abusive relationship. They want no part of a God who would permit or allow it. How can you convince someone that God is a loving God and would allow you to be beaten, bloodied, bruised, and broken? Our Creator, our God, is love. Abuse is not from or of Him. He gave people free will and unfortunately some people choose to be cruel and mean-hearted. There are pastors, ministers, and churches who have supported this ideology over the years. Some are teaching and advising that this is the will of God. If you keep praying and loving the abuser, they will change. The will of God is for you to suffer on this earth for the glory of God. They are taught with 1 Corinthians 13:4-7, *"Love suffers long and is kind; love does not envy; love does not parade itself, is not puffed up; does not behave rudely, does not seek its own, is not provoked, thinks no evil; does not rejoice in iniquity, but rejoices in the truth; bears all things, believes all things, hopes all things, endures all things"*.

We are living with very evil people. Some would rather curse God and die than change. God's Word has been taken and perverted. All we have is the Word of God. God's word has been taught improperly when it allows people to be abused and manipulated.

Beloved, God never intended for you to be abused. That is not His love nor His will for your life. If you reached out to the church for guidance and been told to stay in your abusive marriage, my apologies. I apologize that you were made to feel like the God we serve wanted you to be abused.

In marriage, you put your confidence in each other. You become financially dependent in teamwork. Divorce makes it very difficult at times to have clear thoughts. When you only know your spouse as the provider, it makes it harder to stop hiding the bruises. It may also be hard to get the courage to get out and seek help.

Worrying about your physical welfare in an abusive marriage opens the door to worrying about everything. It will allow doubt to fill your heart about small things. God is not like man. You can trust Him to keep you safe and he will be your provider. Most of all, you can trust His love for you.

I want to share something about the U.S. military and what the Special Operation (S.O. or Special Ops) force does. They're trained at such an intense level in order to be a part of this elite team. Every single member of an aircrew in every military branch must be able to survive on their own. They must be able to handle any environment under any conditions should their aircraft go down. Survival, Evasion, Resistance, and Escape (SERE) is a highly intense program. You are pushed beyond what you thought your limits were. You are taught how to survive if you were kidnapped in another country. This is not a fun program. I have known people who have participated with their branch of the military who never want to experience it again.

A person who is captured and held by an enemy during war is a P.O.W., a prisoner of war. Unfortunately, they are often sexually assaulted, beaten and have body parts amputated. Their bodies undergo trauma. This is a short definition of what a P.O.W. goes through. An abused person is much like a P.O.W. Surviving abuse makes you as strong as one of these Special Force military personnel. You are a warrior. You are a hero to your family and friends. You learned how to live through dreadful situations and were strong enough to make it out.

Congratulations on saving your life and choosing to live! You made an emergency evacuation. Welcome home. The abuse you went through has caused you to be stronger than you ever imagined you could be. I believe you are one strong and tough person that you are not easily defeated. You have wiped your tears after fighting in a great war and received a huge victory - your life.

Learning how to start over from domestic violence is hard. You need to be handled with loving care now. Recovery may be painful, but you will survive! Healing takes time. It is not a race; it is a journey. With God, all things are possible. There are good programs in every community; start there. Talk to a psychiatrist or psychologist. Get therapy to help you understand your process for healing the emotional trauma you experienced. You are not alone. You are not the first person to whom this has happened. Isolation may have been a place you became accustomed to but stay free, unashamed, and learn to socialize again. You deserve a healthy and happy life. You didn't deserve what happened to you. Get connected with a healthy support group. [See Matthew 19:26].

Do not allow the enemy or society to make you feel one ounce of humiliation. Do not blame yourself for the length of time you were in the relationship. Be proud of yourself. Feel good about the fact that you are out. Forgive yourself for being a victim. Forgive yourself if your children were victimized. Release the past and get counseling for your children.

> ✝ *Therefore, there is now no condemnation for those who are in Christ Jesus, because through Christ Jesus the law of the Spirit who gives life has set you free from the law of sin and death.*
>
> Romans 8:1-2

> ✝ *Therefore, if anyone is in Christ, he is a new creation; old things have passed away; behold, all things have become new.*
>
> 2 Corinthians 5:17

Be productive in self-healing. You have to learn things about yourself. Make plans for your future. Setting goals will cause you to have something to achieve. Your future is something to live for. Do not try to bury your feelings with drugs or alcohol. If you survived the abuse by drinking or doing drugs, then get clean and sober.

Fight the temptation to mentally give up on life. Resist all feelings of hopelessness or depression. You will overcome. Revelation 12:11 says, *"We overcome by the blood of the lamb and the word of your testimony."* Let the world know you have survived. You have something to say that could help a person who is where you used to be. Share your story. [See Jeremiah 29:11]. Jesus suffered from abuse.

What type of love is this that would make someone volunteer to be a P.O.W.? Jesus was a P.O.W. in the war against sin. He took that for us and came out with the victory, but it wasn't easy. Jesus was beaten beyond recognition. The Law of Moses said, "No person could receive more than forty stripes because of the severity of the beatings." No human could survive that much force and trauma. It is incomprehensible how much suffering Jesus went through. He was, however, beaten with an instrument known as a flagellum whip.

The Romans scourge instrument was the flagellum. It was designed so that with one lash, flesh would be broken or removed from one's body. A handle was made to fit the hand. It was attached with three leather belts or ropes that had leather thongs made on the belts like spikes. They were knotted with several small pieces of metal, iron, and very sharp pieces forming a ball along the leather. The purpose was to torture, wound, and bring excruciating pain to those being punished. Jesus took this beating not running but standing still in a position where they could easily hit Him. I am sure He fell to His knees with those hits, which would have made it easy for Him to get beaten not only across His back. My guess is, those three leather belts may have hit Him in the back of the head, where they later put a crown of thorns on Him.

They took thorns and made a crown to put over His head. Then they made Him carry huge pieces of wood on His torn open flesh. The wood was believed to be more than forty pounds. He was not only suffering from open wounds and bruises, but blood was also running out from every lash. This was not an easy task. Jesus did this with love. He endured great pain for our atonement. He took upon His flesh every weapon formed against us, every evil act that man has done to you. Every curse that was spoken over you, every time the enemy tried to destroy your confidence, every lie that was told to you, Jesus already paid for it. They were just lies meant to defeat you. Here you are, still standing; you survived when many do not. Now, allow God to give you His rest and His peace. God is about to restore you. Better days, greater moments and years are waiting for you.

You may have been forsaken by a person, by a loved one who promised, "Until death do you part." Jesus did not forsake you. He never will. Jesus is familiar with our pain, sorrow, grief, and sickness. When your heart has felt so broken, so torn into pieces, Jesus felt that too. Hear this, Jesus will heal you from the wounds of abuse. He carried on His own body your diabetes and hypertension. He was beaten for cancer, beaten for lupus, for sickle cell. He was beaten for arthritis. He was beaten for heart conditions. He was beaten for blood disorders, sickness, disease, and every curse known to mankind. Those hard places and uncomfortable situations, He carried them on the cross. Let Him heal you. [See Isaiah 53].

God wants you to go to a new level in your praise and worship. You made it. God will heal you to be able to praise Him for much more. This is a time to just be thankful and praise God for getting you out. Practice being grateful for everything you have. Jesus was the ultimate P.O.W. He died, descended into hell, and was resurrected to give you the ability to survive abuse with victory.

Relocate both physically and mentally if you need to. You do not have to try to rebuild yourself around the corner where your old self lived for years. There are programs that can help you live in another county or state. Give yourself the best opportunity for success and move if you must. [See Psalms 139].

Battered Person Syndrome is a form of post-traumatic stress disorder (PTSD). People who survived abusive relationships often feel like they are still in danger. Fight to get healed. Grab hold to a new title. Be a business owner, entrepreneur, doctor, or lawyer. Do not wear the title, "victim" or "abused" anymore.

You might not be able to see how, where, or who is going to give you money. Step out on faith and get moving. Do not stay and let someone continue to make you afraid. God has made you strong enough to relocate somewhere else.

Rewrite your story. You have the strength to do so. You have the muscles. You can make it. You can go and be free. Do not be co-dependent or limited. Go be your best self. You didn't die by the hand of the abuser, so go and rise above the past. Let that pain develop you to be great.

Helpful Resources

800-799-7233 National Domestic Violence Hotline
www.ncadv.org,
www.safefamilies.com
www.nationalcenterdvtraumamh.org

Readers let's pray

Lord, I thank you for my life, every breath. Thank you for the activity of my limbs. Father, I ask you to lead me to a place of peace and be my shelter. Give me supernatural strength to make it day by day. Deliver me, Lord, from pain and suffering; deliver me from everything that tries to harm me. I put my trust in you. You are my shield. In Jesus' name, Amen.

✝ Declaration

God is with me; He will never leave me nor forsake me.

🎤 Manifesto

I am courageous in the face of conflict
because God is on my side.

🎼 Music

Song: "Pour into Me"
Artist: Atmosphere of Heaven
Album: *Atmosphere of Heaven*, 2012

Song: "Turning Around for Me"
Artist: Vashawn Mitchell
Album: *Created 4 This*, 2002

Song: "I Hope You're ...Praying"
Artist: Kesha
Album: *Rainbow*, 2017

A LITTLE CHAT WITH A BIG GOD

Postscript to Chapter 9

Worry is consuming me. I don't want to live every day paralyzed by fear. I will make a choice today to give up my worries to you. I will make a choice today to say not another day will I live the way I have lived in the past.

I want a brand-new beginning. I believe you can give me that. Today I ask that you forgive me for withholding myself from you, forgive me for my transgressions. I ask that you come into my heart and life. I surrender and make you my God, my Lord. Give me your patience and your strength, so that I can see you are working everything out for me. In Jesus' name, Amen.

Domestic Violence (Emergency Evaluation)

National Hotline numbers to get help.
National Domestic Violence Hotline 800-799-7233

Mental Health
www.mentalhealthamerica.net

CHAPTER 10

Scar Tissue

I had a tear deep inside my rotator cuff that required a shoulder operation. While waiting for the surgery to be approved, I developed scar tissue. Ultimately, the bands of scar tissue limited my ability to move my shoulder with full range. I had a lot of pain, and it became impossible to move it with a full range of motion. This condition is called, "frozen shoulder." I had to have surgery just to remove the scarring issues before they could operate to repair the actual tear. After the surgery, I had to go to physical therapy. This will help to gradually increase mobility and avoid further injury. Physical therapy helps relieve the pain. It will help you regain strength and maximize your new normal. Most importantly, it helps reduce scar tissue from forming.

Scar tissue is our body's natural way of assisting in the healing process. Scar tissue can form around organs and in places that will cause more harm, more pain. Breaking the scar tissue by regularly massaging the area is important to reduce and obviate more scar tissue from forming. If you let scar tissue form around your heart and mind, it can stop you from being healed correctly. It could leave you emotionally and even spiritually disabled.

> ✝ *On that day I will raise up the tabernacle of David, which has fallen down, And repair its damages; I will raise up its ruins, And rebuild it as in the days of old; That they may possess the remnant of Edom, And all the Gentiles who are called by My name, Says the Lord who does this thing.*
> Amos 9:11-12

Scar tissue will harden like a wall around a newly divorced heart. This wall will make you want to throw in the towel. It can cause you to feel like giving up on yourself and on love. Use God's word to break all the hurt away. Do not allow scar tissue to remain. Open yourself up to fasting and praying. Both of these things will massage the deeper scar tissue away. God will complete the good work He started in you. I know you feel discouraged about life. Put the marriage and the divorce in a box and create another life for yourself. Please do not forfeit your dreams nor your promises. Don't allow the scar tissue to paralyze you. You cannot look at past hurt and allow it to predict your future. Stop lingering in the pain from divorce because it will limit future happiness.

God will use what was ruined or destroyed and build it up again. Even the most difficult things you have experienced can be used to make you greater. Even though you've been hurt, you can have a healthy life. Some hurt will propel you into your destiny if you take the bad and use it like a step on a ladder.

> ✝ *Harden not your hearts, as in the provocation, in the day of temptation in the wilderness.*
> Hebrews 3:8 KJV

> ✝ *Forgetting those things which are behind and reaching forward to those things which are ahead, I press toward the goal for the prize of the upward call of God in Christ Jesus.*
>
> Philippians 3:12-14

Turn your attention to what successes you want. It is easy to get caught up on failures, hang-ups, obsessions, and those horrible should haves, would haves, and could haves. That is nothing short of a waste of your valuable time. What will heal the scar tissue is realizing that you might have a little bursitis, tendinitis, or arthritis, but you made it through. Practice in the mirror telling yourself how proud you are of you. Name three things daily that you are proud of yourself for doing. Do that every day for the next ninety days. If you are asking, "Why do I need to do this over and over," It is because you need to invest in yourself. You are worth it. Massage your scar tissue by affirming yourself. Call yourself beautiful or handsome.

Be aware of your body and how you are positioned. Is your head hung low? Are you looking at the ground when you walk? Are you speaking to people and not looking directly into their eyes? Change your body position to have dominion over your environment. Pull your shoulders down. This indicates you are not carrying stress. Do not let them be hunched up to your ears. Stand and sit straight, not curled over. Be aware of your surroundings. Own every footstep you take! Your body posture will either help you feel strong or feel helpless. Walk in a room and look at people – walk with self-confidence. I made it a point to make my outward appearance look great.

Scar tissue left untreated can have you looking a hot mess. I had my hair cute and tried new hairstyles. I put effort into my face and skin daily. I lost weight because

I was exercising on a regular basis. I looked up one day, and inches had come off. The bonus was when I went to the doctor's office and came home with a prize-winning report card. "Miss Eaglin, you are healthy. No borderline conditions to be concerned with." My echocardiogram showed my heart was younger than my age. I didn't wear sadness on my face. I wasn't applying sorrow like it was lipstick or eye shadow. I wanted to look the prettiest I could look.

Your voice needs to be the loudest thing you hear. Find your voice. Do not compare yourself with anyone. Do not be a complainer or critical of everything. Misery cannot be your voice. Take your future and speak life words over it. Tell yourself that you will not procrastinate; you will take every opportunity to advance yourself. The heartache you faced with divorce is one season. It is not the end of your life. Life and death are in the power of the tongue. You will reroute your life away from depression and low self-esteem when you speak the desired result into your life.

The trick of the enemy is to keep you from rejoicing. Rejoice over yourself. You cannot obsess over your divorce and what you lost. Even if you had a prophetic word or dream that said God was going to bring the marriage back. Work on you in the meantime.

It is time to make positive thoughts your default. The most important repetitious thing you can do is re-state manifestos that build you up. Picture your dream life coming to pass like it's going to happen in the next twenty-four hours. Open your mouth and consciously speak to affirm yourself each hour on the hour.

Break the scar tissue by teaching yourself to love you better. Be enthusiastic about who you are and what your future will be. Train your mind to be the birthing ground for your dreams and aspirations. Get fertile, not fallow!

You deserve the best. Start there by saying, "I deserve the best. I will live my most wonderful life. I am successful. I am having a fantastic day. I have joy. I have peace. I have health. I have love. "

If you are in traffic or driving a long distance, practice positive thoughts. No murmuring or complaining about the drive. Say out loud two things you have gratitude about. Think about a new goal. What are some ways you can be creative? How can you spend time with your family creating a great meal? Think about how it feels to play with your kids or imagine the joy of walking your dog. Think of something you want to do that is fun and would cost little to nothing. Think of five uplifting and positive words that describe you.

Use the power that God has given you. Change your life by faith. Even when you do not feel like it, do it by faith. Affirm yourself. Be kind and loving to you. One day at a time walking every step with faith. Take care of yourself better than you have ever taken care of anyone else. You have to take time to be healed. Be healthy physically. Eat a proper healthy diet. Get in shape. Get your annual physical done and know your results. Love the body you are in and be grateful for it.

You have to see yourself as successful, happy, and financially sufficient. Work on evicting all the limiting, demolishing notions about you. The things you can do with your mind and words could revolutionize everything about your life. You are powerful providing you take your thoughts and create the life God said you can have.

Keep your focus on a healthy, positive future. Start your morning with gratitude. What are you thankful for? The fact that you are alive? Start there. Be grateful for your every breath. Sometimes I think over my life and all the things that I have been through, and tears run down my face. I am successful based on the fact that each year it gets better. I am so grateful that despite divorce my life is good. I am thankful for my feet which take me places. I am thankful my nose works! I enjoy smelling flowers and yummy food. I am thankful for what is to come next in my life. Take a few minutes daily and be thankful.

Meditate. Take a minimum of ten minutes to visualize yourself being successful. Actively change your habits. Stop rehearing failures and see yourself obtaining and achieving. By repetition, you will raise your thoughts and rehabilitate your brain.

What are your goals? Do your goals have you aligned with your purpose? Will doing it make you say I am so happy doing this? If your goal is motivated purely by money, it will drive you crazy. You will meet many disappointments because of it.

Listen to your spirit. Are your goals leading you away from God or closer to Him? There are billionaires who are miserable, and there are some who are extremely happy. Most of them say it is because they are not chasing money. They are chasing their dream and living to do their purpose. Don't let fear stop you, fear of success or failure. You learn even if you fail.

Retrain your brain to accept success as a major part of your life. Holding on to the scars will hinder you. It will keep you trapped in regret and emotional pain.

Let's pray.

My God, I thank you for keeping your hands on me. I thank you for rebuilding me, for healing all my brokenness. You gave me the mind of Christ Jesus. I have a sound mind, and I thank you. Lord, bless me with the strength to preserve. I let go of everything I was holding onto. Make me over, Lord. In Jesus' healing name, Amen.

Declaration

I am forgetting those things that are behind me, and I am pressing ahead to my great future.

Manifesto

I am free; nothing hinders me.

Music

Song: "Make Me Over"
Artist: Tonex
Album: *Out of the Box*, 2004

Song: "Trading My Sorrow"
Artist: Darrell Evans
Album: *Freedom*, 1998

A LITTLE CHAT WITH A BIG GOD

Postscript to Chapter 10

I'm tired of being ashamed, humiliated, embarrassed. That's it. I give myself over to you, Lord God. I have done a whole bunch of things that were not good. I ask that you forgive me. I'm going to put my confidence in you. My hope, my trust all in you. I want to be changed. I ask that you give me your wisdom, knowledge, and understanding. In Jesus' name, Amen.

CHAPTER 11

My Weapon

My heart was like shattered glass, scattered in shards. I felt congested with agony in my whole body. In the middle of the mayhem, I was desperate for God to take the heaviness and pain. I began to worship. By accident, I found out just how powerful worship was.

A season of emotional challenges led me in the valley of the shadow of death. You will be tempted to try to fix it with immoral things. To self-medicate on prescription drugs or any drugs and alcohol. Perhaps you want a sexual release with a quick orgasm from someone you're not married to or even from masturbation. That doesn't work since you just get a five-minute pleasure and then days of more regret. People will even try dabbling in the cult spirits to figure out what's going to happen next.

I drank my share of wine. I didn't feel better. I binge-watched reality TV shows, thinking if I watched somebody else's foolery it would make mine seem small in comparison. I tried to numb the pain with a whole bunch of other things. My heart did not feel any better. Then I took myself to the altar and laid myself down. I had to take several seats. An emergency system shutdown of junk. I had to put myself on time-out. Take your pain to the altar. My heart was as low as you can get. I was super lethargic. I went to the doctor. My blood pressure was alarmingly low. That's just how lifeless I was.

Believe God will take your heartache and use it to revive you. With God, you can find the ability to transform your sadness into accomplishments. I believe your pain will produce success if you will go deeper and surrender your pain to God. Draw closer to God in a way that will cause the power within you to be a weapon against the enemy.

Take a worship break. Time to consecrate yourself to the Lord. A time to praise is simply thanking God for what He has done. Worship is thanking God for who He is, who He was, and who He will be tomorrow. First thing I want you to remember is that God is always with you whether you feel Him or not. Worshiping means that you are taking time to acknowledge Him, to meditate and recognize that you are in the presence of the Lord. Make it a private time just between you and God.

Now you have to think about spiritual things that are happening. We have an enemy whom we call the devil. He was originally an angel who oversaw praise and worship. He wanted everything that God had, and he became proud. He wanted to be worshipped. The devil is and was jealous of God. That is why he was kicked out of heaven. He wanted all the adoration, all the glory. He wants to try and take all of us from God. This is just a brief description of the devil. The distractions in your life are the devices of enemy trying to prevent you from breaking free to worship God. I encourage you to read about the father of lies, the devil. [See Ezekiel 28:12-15].

I want you to try every day to spend at least five minutes in meditation to recognize that you're not alone. God is with you. He's right next to you in every situation. Just as you can feel your heartbeat, so too is He right there. As you can feel the breath leave your body, He is right there. Have an attitude of thankfulness that goes into praise and then into powerful worship.

Praise is easy to do every day. Praise God for waking up. Praise God for life, your health, the life of your loved ones. You can run through a list of things to thank God for.

Worship requires dedication and time because you have to first enter into praise. Then lift praise up and go higher in order to worship.

We have to set time away for ourselves in order to worship. To let go of the daily hustle and bustle. The daily worries and confusions, the daily grind. Let it all go. The feelings of despair from divorce. The nagging ache in your heart. You have to put all of those things and people away and come to the throne room.

In theory, it is easy, but it really takes dedication and total surrender to allow yourself to get lost in the moment. I find it easier to worship Him by using all His names.

It is a must to isolate yourself. Allow yourself to temporarily put everything else out of your thoughts. Only think about God. Try to surrender and concentrate. Put your phone on silent. In fact, put it far away from you. Go into a room and close the door behind you. Declare yourself unavailable for five minutes. Eventually, the five minutes will lead to a longer period. You need to start somewhere. When you surrender everything so that you can worship, the devil hears this as shots fired!

Shots fired! If you have the attitude of gratefulness and thankfulness, you create an atmosphere that the enemy cannot be in. It's like being at a gun range, shots are coming from different direction. You don't know exactly where the shots are coming from. That is precisely what your praise and worship does to the enemy. Take your mouth and use it as a spiritual weapon.

Newly single people, you have to make God the "Lover of your Soul." You have to put God in His rightful place, on the throne of your life. If you don't, you might accidentally put something or someone else on the throne of your life. You cannot hear the voice of God clearly when you have a small god and idols in His place.

You have to spend time looking into the face of God. The only way you can see Him is when you surrender and enter into worship. This is a universal principle. You have to learn how to be disciplined with your time. You have to properly learn how to be great with a routine of devotion time to worship God. It is not an overnight magic trick. Spending time in worship will make you live up to your full potential.

Our natural thoughts coupled with our human emotions can have you like a dog chasing its tail. In the process of divorce, you may tend to overthink everything. It is unfortunate, but a lot of people become so scared to move. At times they even sabotage themselves. They entertain procrastinating. I found something that worked to get me out of my head, and that was worshiping God. It is impossible to worry and worship simultaneously.

> ✝ *A man's heart plans his way, But the Lord directs his steps.*
>
> Proverbs 16:9

> ✝ *There are many plans in a man's heart, Nevertheless the Lord's counsel—that will stands.*
>
> Proverbs 19:21

> ✝ *For we know that the law is spiritual, but I am carnal, sold under sin. For what I am doing, I do not understand. For what I will to do, that I do not practice; but what I hate, that I do. But now, it is no longer I who do it, but sin that dwells in me. For I know that in me that is, in my flesh nothing good dwells; for to will is present with me, but how to perform what is good I do not find.*
>
> Romans 7:14-18

Intimacy that is in worship with God shoots down warfare. If you want to feel the consistent presence of God, you have to make time daily to go into worship. Chase after God. There is no man-made comfort, no promotion, no drug high, no orgasm that will totally leave you satisfied like being in the presence of God. God said He seeks a worshiper.

> ✝ *But the hour is coming, and now is, when the true worshipers will worship the Father in spirit and truth; for the Father is seeking such to worship Him. God is Spirit, and those who worship Him must worship in spirit and truth.*
>
> John 4:23-24

Worship gives God all the glory and honor and you are left knowing how powerful you are. When we're walking hand in hand with God, we live a surrendered life. A surrendered life means you humble yourself, acknowledging that everything you have is a gift. That gift was bestowed upon you like your abilities, strengths, and natural talents. Life is a gift. You will hear from heaven if you are humble. Open yourself up to hear. Be still and listen. You will have a heavenly portal—direct connection. In the dry season, in the thirsty days of divorce, you need a direct line to a Heavenly Father who is listening. When your texts go unanswered and you get the voice mail, God's line is always open to you. His voice comes as a strong, impressing, pure feeling.

As I was waiting for my divorce papers, all kinds of challenges were coming at me. I wanted to push every demonic force away from my life. It is easy to get stuck in your own thoughts. How will this go, how will it turn out in court? What will it be like seeing him or her for the first time in a long time? I was stuck and standing in my way rehearsing those what "ifs." What would it look and feel like to be divorced? That question was reoccurring. Often,

I made myself small in my own eyes. I had to shut down my thoughts. I had to discipline myself to sit down, be still, quiet and meditate. Meditating on the fact that I wasn't alone. God was with me. Despite what people would say about divorce, God was with me. God doesn't leave us because we sin. If you blow it in any number of ways, God is still with you.

I had to worship God in spirit and in truth. I felt the peace of God over my mind. It is so easy to meditate on the problems. In worship my thoughts became regulated. I stopped having sleepless nights. The long daydreams that left me anxious disappeared. I stopped reliving the pain. It all came to an end in my worship time. By continuing with a devoted worship time, all the mind games stopped coming. Depression, anxiety, suicidal thoughts – none of those thoughts could come into my time of worship. Do it to keep your mind sane. Do it to get the strength on those weary days.

You will cause things to shift in the atmosphere when you are using this wonderful spiritual weapon of worship. The spirit of truth will guide you out of an endless toxic loop of miserable thoughts.

In mediation time with God I felt my spirit connect and I heard, "When you walk with me, I will show you the short cuts." I was not alone. I felt God was teaching me how to hold on to Him. I didn't wake up and my problems were instantly gone. I stopped being stressed out and felt stronger daily.

The devil's intention is to keep you busy, even doing good Christian stuff or humanitarian things to keep you distracted. Procrastination will grasp you and make you frozen in fear. He cannot hold you up when you live a devoted life as a worshiper. Why don't you load up your weapon and let the enemy of your soul hear shots fired!

I say put an end to feeling miserable, to feeling frustrated, to feeling defeated. Use your worship as a weapon. Begin to let your life reflect God's glory. Rest in His joy and peace that He freely gave you. In the center of your chaos hold on to God. When the hurricane tries to take your roof off, I suggest you worship God. He is in control of your life. When you surrender everything, you will see that the storm of divorce will pass. You will be left standing with your complete sound mind feeling powerful.

Shots fired. When the loneliness of divorce tries to steal your joy, let worship remind you that you are never alone. You will stop fearing being alone and start looking forward to alone time. Isolation will allow you to clearly hear from God. This is a small season in your big life. This needs to be a time of intimacy with Emmanuel, or God is with us. Run to Him when the tears are rolling down your cheeks. Every tear you drop, God catches.

In your meditation worship time, tear down walls that you put up in divorce. Open your heart to allow God to mend you. During those everyday struggles of separation seek the presence of Jesus. In the course of the newness and becoming one person again, let the Lord help you through that process.

In the disarray of divorce, at times you're fighting everything. There are things that just feel too tough to battle. It's like the world is against you. I was there feeling defeated during the day and hopeless at night. I ran to God; I worshiped. I began to feel stronger because my worship had caused my vibe to move in a different direction – one that was delightful. What are you waiting for? It is time to change your direction instead of wasting time and remaining stuck.

✝ *Because of their crime, they cannot escape; in anger, God, strike down the peoples. 8 You have kept count of my wanderings; store my tears in your water-skin — aren't they already recorded in your book? 9 Then my enemies will turn back on the day when I call; this I know: that God is for me. 10 In God — I praise His Word — in Adonai — I praise His Word — 11 in God I trust; I have no fear; what can mere humans do to me?*

Psalms 56:8-12 7 CEB

✝ *So, brothers and sisters, because of God's mercies, I encourage you to present your bodies as a living sacrifice that is holy and pleasing to God. This is your appropriate priestly service. Don't be conformed to the patterns of this world but be transformed by the renewing of your minds so that you can figure out what God's will is—what is good and pleasing and mature.*

Romans 12:1-2 CEB

Practical Application

Study the names of God. Identify how you have seen each name manifest in your life. Jehovah, Jehovah Nissi, Jehovah Shalom, Jehovah Rapha, Jehovah Jireh, Elohim, Adonai, El Shaddai – there are many more.

Readers, we need to pray.

Father God, thank you for being God. I worship you for being wonderful, for being great, for being faithful to me. From this day forward, I will make time to worship you. It is my reasonable service. I need to feel your presence to feel your love all around me daily. I will use my worship to change the atmosphere. In Jesus' transformative name, Amen.

Declaration

My worship is a spiritual weapon.

Manifesto

I make time to be quiet and still
in the presence of my big God.

Music

Song: "I Need Thee Every Hour"
Artist: Annie Hawks

Song: "I Surrender All"
Artist: Various

Song: "Withholding Nothing"
Artist: William McDowell
Album: *Withholding Nothing*, 2013

A LITTLE CHAT WITH A BIG GOD

Postscript to Chapter 11

I need your tender loving compassion, Lord. There has been a whole lot of everything else going on in my world lately. I have done everything my way. I have been the boss; no one could tell me what to do. I had all the answers. This has been to my detriment. Okay. So now I want you to be the boss. I want you to be my Lord. I give you full authority over me. Pardon me of all immoral and disgusting behavior. I put all my trust in you forever. I choose from this day forward to walk after you and for you. In Jesus' name, Amen.

CHAPTER 12

Spiritual Navigation

I was on the freeway, driving into downtown Los Angeles. The traffic has its challenges. This particular day, it was flowing. I was vibin' to some good worship music while praying in the Spirit. Suddenly, I felt led to turn my Global Position System (GPS) on. The GPS directed me to get off the freeway at the next exit. My son taught me to listen to the GPS, even if we have traveled that route before because there may be hazards ahead.

GPS has the latest news and updates, and where construction is on the freeway. It uses satellites and ground stations to stay current. The navigation alerts us to things we cannot see. The Waze navigational app tells us about road debris, potholes and cars parked on the shoulder. If a Waze consumer is passing an issue or accident, they can report it on the Waze app. This type of warning when driving is super helpful.

I got off the freeway. It led me up and down a hill in a residential neighborhood and then back onto the freeway. Once I merged back onto the freeway, in my rearview mirror, there was an accident. Fire trucks were all my eyes could see. Traffic was completely stopped, and no cars were moving. My GPS had warned me early enough that I needed to go a different route. It knew the danger I was headed to and immediately aborted the original driving plan.

We are all seeking direction. Which way should I go? Is this the right time for that plan to go into action? Is there an easier route? What do I need to avoid? Let the Holy Spirit be your GPS. God can download into your thoughts the answers to the questions you need answered. You need to use all your resources when you are moving through life.

You do not have to reinvent the wheel. There are places that you want to go that others have already been. They know how to get there and accomplish it successfully. Why would you spend years trying to do something when you know it has only taken someone else three months to accomplish it? Take the path of least resistance.

To the stubborn spirit, I want to remind you about the children of Israel. They wandered the desert for forty years. The path they traveled should have only taken a few weeks. Stubborn and rebellious actions can delay your blessings and deliver heartaches and disappointment. There is being alive and there is living. Do you want to receive the promise of God now all over your life? Obedience will cause you to reap the blessings of God for your life. Obedience to God will get you to where you want to go a lot quicker. Following God's directions will lead you there with peace and strength for the journey you are traveling.

Spiritual navigation has specific directions for your life. Construct your life in a fashion that is yielding to the Holy Spirit. Let the Holy Spirit be your GPS. I do not want to be in a car broken down on the side of the road trying to figure out how I will get help. Using God's word and insight from the Holy Spirit warns you of danger to come. Be led to living a life that is full and rich.

Embrace God through His Holy Spirit for directions in the divorce process. Divorce at times was like my house being on fire. I stood there in that fire with no clue how to get out. I couldn't breathe. The smoke was consuming me.

I needed a firefighter to go into the smoke-filled building when I could not see my way out. I needed a firefighter to give me oxygen. I went to God and grabbed a hold of Him in the fire. He covered me up with a fireproof spiritual jacket and led me to safety. He did not abandon me. He was right there in the fire with me. He led me out because I trusted hearing His voice. I closed my eyes but opened my faith.

The Holy Spirit

Do you want to receive the promises of God for your life? Ask Him to fill you up with His spirit. Invite the Holy Spirit to come in and live in your heart. Pray to connect to God in a deeper way. Your spirit man knows how to navigate you where God wants you to be. Pray for revelation about your divine destiny. Pray and ask God to download the data of wisdom, knowledge, and understanding of His will for your life. God prepared things for you that people in your life would never expect you to receive. God has revealed it by His spirit. Pray for the Holy Spirit to build you up with power where you feel powerless. In divorce or any other hard times, living under the directions of God will always be the best way to travel.

✝ *Therefore, submit to God. Resist the devil and he will flee from you.*

Philippians 1:6

✝ *I am sure that God Who began the good work in you will keep on working in you until the day Jesus Christ comes again.*

James 4:7

✝ *I will instruct you and teach you in the way you should go; I will counsel you with my eye upon you.*

Psalms 32:8

✝ *The steps of a man are established by the Lord, when he delights in His way.*

Psalms 27:3

✝ *For I know the plans I have for you, declares the Lord, plans for welfare and not for evil, to give you a future and a hope.*
Jeremiah 29:11

✝ *When the Spirit of truth comes, he will guide you into all the truth, for he will not speak on his own authority, but whatever he hears he will speak, and he will declare to you the things that are to come.*
John 16:13

✝ *If any of you lacks wisdom, let him ask God, who gives generously to all without reproach, and it will be given him.*
James 1:5

✝ *Let me hear in the morning of your steadfast love, for in you I trust. Make me know the way I should go, for to you I lift up my soul.*
Psalms 143:8

Holy Spirit Scriptures

✝ *This is the confidence we have in approaching God: that if we ask anything according to His will, he hears us. And if we know that he hears us—whatever we ask—we know that we have what we asked of him.*
1 John 5:14-15

✝ *Let us then approach God's throne of grace with confidence, so that we may receive mercy and find grace to help us in our time of need.*
Hebrews 4:16

✝ *In the same way, the Spirit helps us in our weakness. We do not know what we ought to pray for, but the Spirit himself intercedes for us through wordless groans. And he who searches our hearts knows the mind of the Spirit, because the Spirit intercedes for God's people in accordance with the will of God.*
Romans 8:26-27

Readers Let's Pray.

Lord, I want to go in so many directions. One minute I want to run the next I feel like I can barely crawl. If I ask a lot of people for directions with my life I will have too many voices in my head. I need you to give me directions. You created me and you know what path I should walk in. Order my steps, I will follow you my Shepherd.

✝

Declaration
My GPS is God's word.

Manifesto

My spirit yields to God.

Music

Song: Take Me There
Artist: Anna Golden
Album: Take Me There, 2016

Song: Holy Spirit
Artist: Francesca Battistelli
Album: If We're Honest

Song: Order My Steps
Artist: Barbara Johnson Tucker
Album: Order My Steps, 1992
Awards: Best New Album 1997

A LITTLE CHAT WITH A BIG GOD

Postscript to Chapter 12

I have been told so many lies about myself and my life. I do not even recognize myself. I come today asking you to wash me in truth. Guide me in your truth. Lead me. I need a big God in my life right now, always. I confess with my mouth that you are Lord. Jesus, you have redeemed me. Give me your instructions. Forgive me of the things that I have done that are not pleasing in your eyes. Bring me out of distress. I will follow your holy Word all the days of my life. In Jesus' name, Amen.

CHAPTER 13

Tearing Down Idols

There is a divine order in which God expects us to live by - God, our spouse, our children, the church etc. When this order is taken out of context, it opens doors for issues and sometimes happens without even realizing it. The moment our spouse becomes our idol. There is no other way to describe it. I was so caught up in the process of making my marriage a success that the successes and failures had consumed me.

I cringe to say it, but my marriage had become a god. I woke up thinking about it. I went to bed thinking about it. My marriage was the first thing in my life. My thoughts of a failing marriage were unbearable. My thoughts were distorted about marriage. Almost all my prayers, regardless of how they started, all went back to something for him or for our marriage. My worship to God would start the same way but end with me telling God all about my husband or marriage. Was I wrong, was I doing marriage and being a wife out of order? I would scratch my scalp wondering. During the separation thoughts of failure just kept penetrating my brain.

A girlfriend reminded me that I wasn't off balanced nor was I worshiping my husband. I was doing what the Bible instructed a wife to do. A single woman and a wife have different roles. She assured me I had stepped into the role of wife. I needed that validation to allow my head to heal. 1 Corinthians 7:32-34 teaches, "But I want you to be free from concern. The unmarried man is concerned about the things of the Lord, how he may please the Lord; but the married man is concerned about worldly things, how he may please his wife, and his interests are divided. The unmarried woman or the virgin is concerned about the matters of the Lord, how to be holy and set apart both in body and in spirit; but a married woman is concerned about worldly things, how she may please her husband".

When I first got married, I wanted to be the best wife and please my husband. Nowadays being the best spouse is not everyone's objective. I am from Louisiana. Principles of marriage instilled in me were traditional. A woman's place is to take care of their home. To be a pleasing wife. Women worked and took care of her home. I had heard, preached, and taught messages on a supportive spouse concept. I remember being a kid sitting in the room with grown women hearing my mom and other ladies talk about the woes of being a wife. A woman should go above and beyond for the success of a marriage. This is pleasing to God, as long as we are not doing things that are immoral or illegal. Trying to be like our parents or our ideal of marriage can quickly drive you insane.

> ✝ *A wife of noble character who can find? She is worth far more than rubies. Her husband has full confidence in her and lacks nothing of value. She brings him good, not harm, all the days of her life. She selects wool and flax and works with eager hands. She is like the merchant ships, bringing her food from afar. She gets up while it is still night; she provides food for her family and portions for her female servants.*

She considers a field and buys it; out of her earnings she plants a vineyard. She sets about her work vigorously; her arms are strong for her tasks. She sees that her trading is profitable, and her lamp does not go out at night. In her hand she holds the distaff and grasps the spindle with her fingers. She opens her arms to the poor and extends her hands to the needy. When it snows, she has no fear for her household; for all of them are clothed in scarlet. She makes coverings for her bed; she is clothed in fine linen and purple. Her husband is respected at the city gate, where he takes his seat among the elders of the land. She makes linen garments and sells them and supplies the merchants with sashes. She is clothed with strength and dignity; she can laugh at the days to come. She speaks with wisdom, and faithful instruction is on her tongue. She watches over the affairs of her household and does not eat the bread of idleness. Her children arise and call her blessed; her husband also, and he praises her: "Many women do noble things, but you surpass them all." Charm is deceptive, and beauty is fleeting; but a woman who fears the Lord is to be praised. Honor her for all that her hands have done, and let her works bring her praise at the city gate.

Proverbs 31:10-31

I wanted to be that Proverbs 31 woman and make sure if my husband had a need that (if it were in my power), I could meet that need. I broke myself trying to advance my family. As a wife I went out of my way trying to make things happen. I ultimately wanted him to have the best from clothes to cars.

Out of Balance

I allowed my thoughts to solely focus on how to be a good wife. My impression of what a good wife should look like was southern traditional. I believed in the cooking of three regular meals each day or at least making him a lunch to take with him. I believed in serving and cleaning. With consistency, I tried to keep the romance alive and well. I did this with love notes, pictures, videos. I wanted him to feel my love for him. Writing that little special note for him to find with his lunch. We are a texting generation. Sending some cute or sexy text to the man you are married to are all acceptable.

When the marriage hit a wall, I was seeking to find what else I could do to make this marriage work. How can I do more things to make him love me? What could I do to keep the marriage great? How did I need to behave in order to keep from arguing, to seek to understand him and his needs? I was seeking God but not putting God first. There was a moment I was asking God to show my husband that he was first and how much I loved him. Look at how my mind worked. My priorities were off balance. Even when I was reaching out to God, I was acknowledging that this man – this marriage – was important to me.

Being estranged from your spouse sometimes feels like life is not worth living. This could be a sign that you have made some idols in your life. If God does not remain on the throne of your life, you will not hear Him speak clear direction to you. God was Lord over everything until I fell in love and got married. God needs to be more important than anything you are going through. Try not to make your divorce an idol. Condemning yourself like you failed God. The divorce did not take God by surprise. If you thought your prayers could change the other person that is not how prayer works. God alone changes the heart of people. He made people to have free choice to listen. Forgive yourself if you thought for one minute that you were the savior of your marriage. I felt for a short time that I had failed God. I believed that since I was the one with more spiritual knowledge, I should have been able to stand and defeat all attacks against the marriage. I hear people say things like, "I was the best thing that ever happened to them. I made them who they are today. If it wasn't for me, they would not have nothing." You may have a savior complex. This leaves no room for God to be God.

The jealous God shook my world. He loves us so much. He never wants His children to be walking in error. I had that quick "ugh" feeling from the Holy Spirit that I was so far off track. The devil will distort what was meant to be done in service to God. He will pollute everything if we are not careful.

We make idols in the most innocent ways even trying to build our self-esteem up. As a result, you could start filling yourself with unhealthy, evil, sexual or selfish desires, or start using people to get what you want because you are trying to fix the hole in your heart without God.

Out of balance is how we begin to ask anyone who will listen to us for advice if we have God in the wrong place in our life. By having the King of Kings in the wrong place, the door is wide open for the Devil to waltz on in. You will feel defeated, even want to let everything go. The problem will have you bound and weigh you with unnecessary baggage and feelings. Your business is to trust God. Surrender your life and thoughts. This means ask God for direction or to at least bless what you are doing. Surrendering to God is a daily activity. Trusting in God is hard when you don't know how things will work out. Relying on Him is a reminder that you are never alone. This process of trusting God can feel unsettling, and even uncomfortable. The more you do it, the feeling of ease will grow. You'll start seeing things differently when you stop thinking you have to come up with the solution. In everything, God is in total control.

Single Again

Now it is time to return to a position to please God. I no longer have a husband to please; I get to be daughter again. In the same way some young adults return home from college or if their path just led them back home. What a very comforting feeling to return home. I might not have a husband, but I have a protector and provider; God, the loving father waiting for me to turn my attention back to him.

When we allow doubt and fear to dictate our movement, we may not feel strong. As a newly single person, it is easy to begin to feel like you will live life on your own terms. You have no one to answer to. You can sabotage your future that way. Jumping into new relationships without allowing yourself to grieve and heal. Choosing to live your life based on the article in some fashion magazine or reality show. Respect your body. Love yourself in a productive way that will generate no regrets.

There is plenty of fun to be had. I'm not saying be single and a hermit living in solitude because you are divorced, I'm saying make good choices. Analyze all your actions and examine the consequence. You are not punishing your ex-spouse by what you do, who you kiss and go out with.

The truth is, they might not even be thinking about you. I didn't follow my ex-spouse on social media. I needed to heal. This might crush your ego my friend, knowing that you may not cross their mind. They may have gone on without one thought of your feelings. This is the advice you will get on social media or watching television shows. You can prove to them how large you are living, or how quickly you recovered by getting another lover. Horse poop! Do not concern yourself with what the ex-spouse thinks nor others. Reckless deeds will have you finding yourself crying over the big mess you bring to your life by trying to rapidly appear to be over your marriage.

Surrender and rip down any altar you have made by putting your singleness above God and thinking, "It's all about me now," or "The best way to get over a person, is to be underneath another." Put God as the head of your life. It's time to tear down any thoughts and actions you may participate in that does not make you a better person. Remove anything that has you out of the will of God. Tear them down.

Scriptures to help avoid the pitfalls of being single.

✝ *Surely God is my help; the Lord is the one who sustains me. Submit to Him being the final authority of your life.*
Psalms 54:4

✝ *Submit yourselves, then, to God. Resist the devil, and he will flee from you. Come near to God and He will come near to you. Wash your hands, you sinners, and purify your hearts, you double-mind.*
James 4:7-8

✝ *For the Word of God is alive and active. Sharper than any double-edged sword, it penetrates even to*

dividing soul and spirit, joints and marrow; it judges the thoughts and attitudes of the heart. Nothing in all creation is hidden from God's sight. Everything is uncovered and laid bare before the eyes of Him to whom we must give account.
Hebrews 4:12-13

We have been given grace and faith to receive all of God's promises. Falling in love and being married is meant to be wonderful. Unfortunately, you know that women/men can leave or forsake you, but not this wonderful God we serve. Where would we be without God? We soon find out when we build altars in our lives and name them spouses, marriage or any other thing.

† *You shall have no other gods before me. "You shall not make for yourself an image in the form of anything in heaven above or on the earth beneath or in the waters below. You shall not bow down to them or worship them; for I, the Lord your God, am a jealous God, punishing the children for the sin of the parents to the third and fourth generation of those who hate me, but showing love to a thousand generations of those who love me and keep my commandments.*
Exodus 20:3-6

† *Do not worship any other god, for the Lord, whose name is Jealous, He is a jealous God.*
Exodus 34:14

The interpretation of these scriptures is that God is speaking to His church, His bride. He is saying do not cheat on me. Do not put anything above our relationship, our marriage. He is saying I am the lover of your soul. Do not forget from where all these blessings flow. I take good care of you, my bride. I am your protector. I am your healer. I am your deliverer. I adorn you with good gifts. Only God alone should get our worship. Loving other things or people before God is not what he wants us to do. In our relationship, as the bride, which is how God views us, we are supposed to cleave to our marriage with God. We must remain faithful to Him. We are not allowed to let anything be inserted on the altar above God. If we take our affections or our worship and give it to our anything or anyone, we are wrong. Those things are temporarily fulfilling, yielding fleeting happiness.

Rip down any altar you have made with your spouse or the marriage. Put God as the head of your life. Confess with your mouth that He is Lord over everything that concerns you. Ask God to forgive you for putting things higher than him for idolatry. Doing this is a huge step of saying, "I trust you with my life God."

Readers, we pray.

Lord, I have put people and other things before you, and for that I am sorry. I won't do it again. You are Lord of Lords. I submit to you; I resist the devil; therefore, he must flee. With my whole life I will serve you. I will keep you in the throne of my life. In Jesus' name, Amen.

Declaration

I submit to you as Lord over every area of my life.

Manifesto

I will only serve one God, the great I Am.

Music

Song: "Because of Who You Are"
Artist: Martha Munizzi
Album: *Say the Name*, 2002
Awards: Dove Award Nominations

Song: "Nobody Like You, Lord"
Artist: Maranda Curtis
Album: *Maranda Experience*, 2017
Awards: Dove Award Nomination

A LITTLE CHAT WITH A BIG GOD

Postscript to Chapter 13

Today I recognize that I am lost. I am trying to figure out my place in life, but I am paralyzed with fear. I want you to come and be with me today and forever, Lord. Direct me, Lord. I believe that you are my Savior. Jesus, I am asking that you come and live in my heart. Help me with my daily activities. I want wisdom; I want your guidance. I want the boldness and courage that I have heard only you can provide. I receive your grace and mercy for the journey. Thank you for my freedom. In Jesus' name, Amen.

CHAPTER 14

Temporary Season

When fall comes, the leaves on the trees begin to change. Where there once was green, we see brown. The blooming flowers wither. We put away our bright floral colors. Daylight savings time changes: darkness comes early. Before you know it, even the temperature has changed. Sweaters and scarves return to our closets. I look forward to this time of the year because I know my favorite holidays are approaching. Schools take a break, and children are at home. It is a time where families get together to celebrate and enjoy quality time. The cameras come out, and memories are recorded and posted.

The day will come when you have to spend that first holiday as a divorced person. As for me, I ran to family. I wanted to be surrounded with love. I allowed myself to be with safe people. It might be a friend that is like family. I hope you lean on someone during the holidays. Especially if you have small children. The way you handle the holidays will greatly affect them. Sometimes we have to make sacrifices. Do your best to give your children a wonderful holiday. The weather makes the day gloomy enough. Our little children should be able to experience cheer and joy in the house.

It could be very hard during the holidays, so plan out how you can have a successful time. Take time to write down your plans and things you want to do. Being able to see the image of things you want to do will redirect your thoughts. This will give you time to pray for strength. Try to be with supportive people. Plan to do things that will make you laugh and bring good new memories. Avert your thinking from terror and apprehension to affirmation and happiness.

Include your children on the decision-making for activities and events on how you will spend your time. Be ready to make some compromises for the good of the family. This will make everyone look forward to a good time. It is okay if you have to go outside and catch your breath during the holiday party. When you take that five minutes to be alone and regroup your emotions, spend that time recalling things you are grateful for. You always want to use thankfulness to combat emotional hurt.

When the holiday season comes around, the devil really tries to steal a person's strength and joy. He tries to make it his time of year. During the first year, you may feel lonely, even helpless or hopeless. These are all tricks of the devil. He wants to fill you with regrets. He would like to make memories of the marriage play over all the historical moments. End the cycle and know you have a real pure love holding you in this temporary season. The love of God will supply you and support you. Love is all around you. Focus on getting healed from brokenness and free from bondage. It takes a lot of work to keep yourself mentally healthy. It takes an aggressive amount of work to forge ahead and be victorious.

> ✝ *I beseech you therefore, brethren, by the mercies of God, that you present your bodies a living sacrifice, holy, acceptable to God, which is your reasonable service, And do not be conformed to this world, but be transformed by the renewing of your mind, that you may prove what is that good, and acceptable and perfect will of God.*
>
> Romans 12: 1-2

> ✝ *Therefore, having been justified by faith, we have peace with God through our Lord Jesus Christ, through whom also we have access by faith into this grace in which we stand, and rejoice in hope of the glory of God.*
>
> Exodus 34:14

Physical Rest

> *Dictionary's definition of tired: A feeling or showing of weariness, especially because of over-exertion or a lack of sleep. Tired, worn out, spent, exhausted, fatigued – in other words, dog-tired!*

In our American society, we work seven days per week. If we work the typical five weekdays, add on the weekend for family obligations or a heavy social life, and we are super busy. We rarely get the rest our bodies need because we never stop long enough to rest. Being tired is a terrible thing. Some people overexert themselves. They become so tired they are unable to go to sleep.

The problem with operating tired and sleep deprived is you are not working at your best. Studies show that driving sleepy is like driving drunk. You do not see everything you should, and your reaction time is slowed down. You throw your body systems off. Your pH levels and hormones become unbalanced, and your brain suffers chemical imbalance. Your immune system becomes vulnerable. It is necessary to rest and recalibrate. Do not give your life less than 100%. Get the rest your body needs. You need maximum strength and efforts to propel you to your destiny.

> ✝ *And on the seventh day God ended His work which He had done, and He rested on the seventh day from all His work which He had done. Then God blessed the seventh day and sanctified it, because in it He rested from all His work which God had created and made.*
>
> Genesis 2:2-3

> ✝ *And He said to them, "Come aside by yourselves to a deserted place and rest a while." For there were many coming and going, and they did not even have time to eat. So, they departed to a deserted place in the boat by themselves.*
>
> Mark 6:31-32

> ✝ *For we do not want you to be ignorant, brethren, of our trouble which came to us in Asia: that we were burdened beyond measure, above strength, so that we despaired even of life.*
>
> 2 Corinthians 1:8

In the scriptures we see very powerful men of God. People, in fact, that God had chosen. They did notable things in the Bible. These men had an ear for the voice of God. They walked with God; they spoke to God. God blessed these men. Yet, even with all that they did, at times they felt like dying. They felt like giving up. They too dealt with grief and mourning.

Grief and Mental Health

Excessive grief has been labeled by society as depression; a condition dealing with mental illness. I wanted you to see it in the Bible because life can make you question your sanity. Have you felt like throwing in the towel and saying to God I do not want to anymore? This is unfair! Listen, I get it. I have felt that. Grief is painful, and it hurts. It makes us walk with our heads down in sorrow. It makes us physically tired. It is the emotion we feel when we lose someone not only to death but divorce. A marriage dying represents the painful death of your friendship with your spouse, the painful death of your family unit, the painful death of an important dream.

Losing your marriage opens you up to a season of grief. When we do not deal with our emotions properly, we experience depression and feelings of severe despondency. Dejection and self-doubt creep in which swiftly turn to serious depression. Depression is a common but urgent medical illness that negatively affects how you feel, the way you think, and how you act. Fortunately, it is also treatable. Depression causes feelings of sadness and or a loss of interest in activities once enjoyed. I know I addressed depression in an early chapter, but it is a vital topic. I wanted to expose more details of it so that you can be healed.

If you are experiencing depression, it is okay to get a professional therapist. There are certain life traumas that are just so difficult, we need outside help. If you found a lump growing on your body, you would run to the doctor. If you were diagnosed with diabetes and your doctor told you to take medicine, you would. How you were raised to view mental health or psychologists will be a factor in how you view getting help. There are a lot of negative stigmas regarding seeing a psychologist, especially in certain cultures. Pride could be a factor as well. You own the key to every area of your life. Don't just survive but be free. Get the help you need. Just do it.

The church has not spoken enough about mental health. We need to pray and apply the Word - that is what the church teaches. We need to use faith, prayer, and trust in God for any sickness. This is true, but we also should consider going to a psychologist for counseling. Look at mental health as a sickness that has manifested in your head. It's no different than sickness that can show up in your body, like cancer or hypertension. Your mind needs a checkup just like the rest of your body.

I went to a psychologist for counseling. A psychologist does not give medicine. They work with you to identify practical things you can do to help with any mental health issues. I believe with the help and advice from my psychologist, I healed quicker and more effectively. If you need medication, then you can seek the help of a psychiatrist. The church ministers may try counseling you. However, I recommend a person who is a board certified, licensed therapist.

> ✝ *Therefore, the king said to me, "Why is your face sad, since you are not sick? This is nothing but sorrow of heart." So, I became dreadfully afraid.*
> Nehemiah 2:2

> ✝ *Reproach has broken my heart, And I am full of heaviness; I looked for someone to take pity, but there was none; And for comforters, but I found none.*
> Psalms 69:20

> ✝ *Hope deferred makes the heart sick, but when the desire comes, it is a tree of life.*
> 2 Corinthians 1:8

Spiritual depression can open the door for the devil. It also opens us up to a spirit of heaviness. Fight to keep yourself from being depressed. No matter how much we loved what we lost, we have to decide to trust God. Let God into your life. Allow God to fill you with joy. He has plans for you. They are good and not of evil. He wants you to enjoy life and have fun. Know that God is protecting you. God's love will keep you from dangers you can see and those you are unaware of.

Time to Heal

Let the loss go by learning to live in your new chapter. Ultimately you have to stop crying over it. Stop being bitter. Stop being angry. Stop being in denial. It is time to accept the loss, so you can LIVE, so you do not die to depression. If it is a death of a loved one, we learn by leaning on God to live. You never get over someone you have loved. However, God will teach you how to live with it day by day. Even when we bury our loved one, we have a time for mourning. Eventually you must welcome the season of joy back into your life. Let the loss of the marriage go. At some point you have to say farewell to the marriage, so you can continue to truly live.

While waiting for the paperwork for my divorce, I fought hard not to deal with some of my emotions. One day I heard God say, "I want you to stop everything and let me heal you. You are tired and making mistakes."

I told God, "No thanks, that sounds like work." I would rather be healed supernaturally please. God let me know I needed to be healed not just from the current pain. God, our great physician, wanted to get to the root of the pain. The place where I had originally been hurt but not healed. Getting to where the root began would allow the cycle to end. You should not base big life decisions on temporary emotions from a temporary season in your life.

I went days still trying to avoid the process of getting to the source of my brokenness. It is easy to say you want to have a new life and spouse in the future. You must be willing to do the hard work. You have to look at your life with a magnifying glass. I had to examine myself. There were unresolved issues still present. The deep wounds had only been bandaged.

After a week of being sick to my stomach, I said, "Okay God, I hear you." I took time off work and allowed myself to go through the process. Fasting and praying was my priority and a must for my wounds to be healed. I stopped watching television and social media. I was not available for talking on the telephone. I prayed and listened. You cannot be afraid of the silence. I discovered unresolved pain. Words that had been spoken over my life as a girl in my teenage years had left broken pieces and small tears in my soul. It grew as I grew, shaping me to doubt my abilities, talents, and strengths. Damage to my self-esteem if left untreated by God, could have left me with a disability forever. Low self-esteem was causing me to have an unfulfilled life. Take the time you need to soul search.

Are there somethings you have in your life loading you down like past hurts? Have you been carrying childhood hurt, rejections, prejudice, hateful words spoken over your life? It is mandatory to release the junk, the pain, the hang-ups. You need to free yourself. Release it! Don't let anything continue to cripple you.

Recommended Activities

1. Gratitude strengthens our emotions; being thankful brings health to our bodies; gratitude gives us hope. Practice gratitude. It can remove depression. Daily think about what you have; be thankful for it all and say it out loud. For everything big or small. This will help you overcome a spirit of heaviness.
2. Daily exercise. Go for a walk at lunch; eat outside to get some sunlight; look at a rose; marvel over the flowers and the trees; listen to the birds singing.
3. If comedians make you laugh, then open up Netflix and get to laughing. Don't let the devil steal your joy. A joyless life is not the life of a believer. Hold fast to the joy of the Lord.
4. Scream. Get all the pain out. Just let it go.

✝ *To proclaim the acceptable year of the Lord, And the day of vengeance of our God; To comfort all who mourn, To console those who mourn in Zion, To give them beauty for ashes, The oil of joy for mourning, The garment of praise for the spirit of heaviness; That they may be called trees of righteousness, The planting of the Lord, that He may be glorified.*
Isaiah 61:2-3

✝ *Therefore, having been justified by faith, we have peace with God through our Lord Jesus Christ, through whom also we have access by faith into this grace in which we stand, and rejoice in hope of the glory of God.*
Romans 5:1-2

✝ *To them God willed to make known what are the riches of the glory of this mystery among the Gentiles: which is Christ in you, the hope of glory.*
Colossians 1:27

Readers let's pray.

Lord, I thank you for my life and a sound mind. Father, where you lead me, I will follow. I know your plans for me are far better than those of my own. Take me where you want me to be. Open doors of opportunities for me and never leave me alone. In Jesus' name, Amen.

✝ Declaration

My life and times are in your hand.

🎤 Manifesto

I submit to the leading of the Holy Spirit.

🎵 Music

Song: "Total Praise"
Artist: Richard L. Smallwood
Album: *Adoration*, 1996

A LITTLE CHAT WITH A BIG GOD

Postscript to Chapter 14

I have been told so many lies about myself and my life. I do not even recognize myself. I come today asking you to wash me in truth. Guide me in your truth. Lead me. I need a big God in my life right now. Always. sI confess with my mouth that you are Lord. Jesus, you have redeemed me. Give me your instructions. Forgive me of the things that I have done which were not pleasing in your eyes. Bring me out of my distress. I will follow your holy word all the days of my life. In Jesus' name, Amen.

CHAPTER 15

Living Victorious After Divorce

As we come to the close, I want to remind you that all it takes is faith in God to bring forth God's supernatural power, favor, and healing. Expectations are the breeding ground for God's miracles. Victory belongs to you. Never stop improving yourself. You deserve the best life you can live. Keep your heart open, so rich love can always fill it. Divorce brings hard unexpected life changes. After the pain, you have to welcome starting over. Be glad and excited about the new you. You are a great sight to see!

With God nothing is impossible. Faith in God and in yourself will open the door for victory. The Lord has blessed your life. In God's eyes you are special. Going forward, you have to think highly of yourself. Line your thoughts up to God's word. You are a winner. You are victorious. You are not a loser.

You will triumph and overcome in other chapters of your life if you continue with these principles. Make your life and everything around you beautiful. Walk in the room and change the atmosphere. Be the sunshine.

Look at this scripture in the book of Samuel. Here we see David, a mighty warrior leading his army home from a victory. He arrives to find unexpected heartache, confusion, and disappointment.

The enemy had come when he least expected and taken his wife and kids. His soldiers' families were gone as well. David cried. He felt the pain of the loss just like you. Then David prayed to the Lord. He wanted to go and get what the enemy had stolen. God answered David. He said, "Go pursue and you will recover all."

> ✝ *Now it happened, when David and his men came to Ziklag, on the third day, that the Amalekites had invaded the South and Ziklag, attacked Ziklag and burned it with fire, and had taken captive the women and those who were there, from small to great; they did not kill anyone, but carried them away and went their way. So David inquired of the Lord, saying, "Shall I pursue this troop? Shall I overtake them?" And He answered him, "Pursue, for you shall surely overtake them and without fail recover all.*
>
> 1 Samuel 30:1-2, 8

David and his soldiers must have felt defeated. God told him to go and pursue, and he would recover all. This is not how it ended for David. He pursued and recovered everything that was ripped away from him. He went on to enjoy his reign as king.

Need I remind you, Greater is He that is inside of you than he that is in the world. No matter how dysfunctional life may have been, God will perfect things that were wrong and make them new and improved.

You have resurrection power living inside of you. Rise up from whatever coffin divorce tried to put you in. No, you are not dead or a failure. Silly people doubted your God-given abilities. Our bible tells us *"If God be for us, who can stand against us"* (See Romans 8:11).

† *We are more than conqueror through Christ Jesus.*
　　　　　　　　　　　　　　　　　　　　　Romans 8:28

The cross, Calvary, assures you that you win. Stand in your warrior pose. Stand in the mirror and put your hands in your victory position. I win! This has to be your outlook on life. I am living proof this will make all the difference.

† *Therefore, take up the whole armor of God that you may be able to withstand in the evil day, and having done all, to stand. Stand there-fore, having girded your waist with truth, having put on the breastplate of righteousness, and having shod your feet with the preparation of the gospel of peace; above all, taking the shield of faith with which, you will be able to quench all the fiery darts of the wicked one. And take the helmet of salvation, and the sword of the Spirit, which is the Word of God.*
　　　　　　　　　　　　　　　　　　Ephesians 6:13-17. ESV

Keep filling yourself with affirming things that feed your self-image. The first place you must win the battle is in your mind. No plan of the devil towards your life will ever cause you to lose. Wake up daily with the mind of Christ Jesus. Here is what that means for every negative thought that comes to your mind, you must remind yourself that you have the victory *"Let this mind be in you, which was also in Christ Jesus"* (Philippians 2:5 KJV).

You were made in God's own image. You are a powerful being. Do something with all that power and greatness. Choose to live a better life daily. Defeat the enemy in your mind and purify your thoughts. You will not be destroyed.

Remember ... you can make it. God is with you. He takes you out of the miry clay, known also as the crazy places of life. I am talking sewer funky crap. You can fall in a pile of manure, but He loves you so much He will clean you up. Reading the Word of God reminds you that God always restores you.

The devil is like a roaring lion. He is most certainly not a real lion. He is just a small powerless ant with a microphone and a huge sound system. Take your mind and fill yourself up with positive energy. You have to see yourself as unbreakable. [See Ephesians 4:27 and Psalms 8:6]. Affirm yourself daily.

We fall down sometimes. Look up and always pull yourself back up. We go through the tough times. I know they can be really terrible, times of sickness, loss, grief, even the death of those we loved. Still stand back on your feet and dust yourself off. Stand up straight; get in your warrior pose and look at yourself in the mirror. Say it loudly, so even I can hear you: I am unbreakable and undefeated; I will live victoriously.

God is going to supersize your life with blessings. Still to come, you will experience redemption, compensation, restoration, and elevation. Let this experience cause you to dig deep within yourself to pull your purpose out. Do everything in your ability to live out the life you want for yourself. Keep your trust in God. Remember divorce is just one chapter of your big life. You have numerous victories waiting for you.

I personally know that everything that I have shared with you has placed me in a position to say to you today that I am living victoriously after divorce!

Thank you for spending your time reading this book. I hope it has touched your life in some significant way. Please, don't keep it to yourself. Tell others who need to be blessed by my story. Also, be sure to follow me on social media and drop me a line to let me know how this book has helped you.

Practical Applications

1. Write what your purpose is.
2. Identify how to operate to your full capacity in your purpose.
3. Create a vision board of the things you want to accomplish or possess.
4. Take the class, obtain certifications, degrees or licenses, think outside the box.

Dear, Victorious Person,
let's turn to prayer together one final time.

Thank you, God, for redeeming me. Thank you, God, that I have survived divorce because of you. I run to you, Father; take me to my better life. You said in your Word that you came so I can have life and that more abundantly. I trust you with my whole heart that you will do just that. Thank you for calling me your own child; thank you for love that washes over me. In Jesus' name, Amen.

✝ Declaration

I have victory.

🎤 Manifesto

I start. I finish. I accomplish.

𝄞 Music

Song: "Worth Fighting"
Artist: Brian Courtney
Album: *Worth Fighting*, 2015

Song: "Great is Your Mercy:
Artist: Donnie McClurkin
Album: *Live in London,* 2000
Song: "Victory Belongs To Jesus"
Artist: Various

A LITTLE CHAT WITH A BIG GOD

Postscript to Chapter 15

Wow, I have read and heard about how good you are. How you press the restart button on people's lives. I see now that what I thought was the end really can be a new beginning. I want what I have seen and heard. I want victory in my life. I have been holding on to resentment and lack of forgiveness, but I let it go now. Lord, I want what you have for me. I want a God who walks with me in life. I have decided to make you my only God. Wash away my wrongdoing and teach me a new way to live. In Jesus' name, Amen.

In Loving Memory

Sometimes isolation is a response to your pain, because it forces you to push people away. We didn't divorce because we didn't love each other. We divorced because we couldn't stand the pain that loving each other was causing. God used you to make me a better person, better woman and mother. God put you in my life, it helped me heal from old scars and pain I had never dealt with. Love gave me a new peace and laughter. Selah. The joy of loving and the pain of losing you. I know that the memory of our love will always be with me.

> Song: "Till We Meet Again"
> Artist: Kirk Franklin
> Album: *Kirk Franklin and the Family* 1993

> Additional Song Information
> God Be with You Till We Meet Again
> Jeremiah E. Rankin, 1828–1904
> Music: William G. Tomer, 1833–1896

SUZÁNNE EAGLIN is an author, entrepreneur, minister of the gospel, and motivational speaker. Her 12-year career in law enforcement is a motivating force towards her strong empathic feelings and activist tendencies. As a survivor of trauma, she has devoted the last 18 years to helping others. It is her mission to uproot dysfunction and replace it with healing, power, and love.

Suzánne continues to focus on uplifting the downtrodden. Currently, she serves as a board member for Lead Your Ship Non Profit. Amongst her proudest accomplishments is her 26-year-old son, Elijah Miskel and authoring her first book, *Living Victoriously After Divorce*. She is excited to share her personal testimony with her community. Her talking points include:

- The five stages of grief as experienced by the divorced heart
- The emotional trauma consequently experienced in the dissolution of a marriage
- Practical steps toward recovery and even renewed empowerment

Suzánne approaches each event with authenticity and transparency. The chief of her messages is, "Divorce is not the end of the world." She explains how to remove doubt reclaim your power within, refine your life's vision, and take back your joy. Suzánne shares secrets of building a new foundation for a healthier life free from anger and bitterness. She teaches how to wake up to happiness, set ordered goals, and visualize victory. It is her aim to help everyone involved in the process of divorce, including the children. In short, this powerful speaker will move you and your community toward wholeness.

Follow me on Facebook, Instagram and YouTube.
Suzánne Eaglin

For group purchases, book signing, engagements and more, please visit:
www.livingvictoriouslyafterdivorce.com

Made in the USA
Middletown, DE
02 May 2021